Due

Tramping Through the Trilliums

A Satirical History of Ontario

by

Orland French

illustrated by

Philip Mallette

This book was written and produced without any subsidy, loan, gift, Wintario grant, or other form of financial assistance from the Government of Ontario. Which is why it's been so much fun.

Canadian Cataloguing in Publication Data

French, Orland.
  Tramping through the trilliums

ISBN 0-458-97920-1

1. Ontario - History - Anecdotes, facetiae, satire, etc. I. Title.

FC3061.3.F74 1984   971.3'002'07   C84-098573-8
F1057.5.F74 1984

Printed and bound in Canada

1 2 3 4 84 88 87 86 85

Contents

Salting the Porridge
· AN INTRODUCTION ·

Imagine dropping a big saucepan of porridge at North Bay. Watch it ooze across the map. See it mush towards Manitoba. See it congeal around the Great Lakes. See it glop along Quebec's border. Ontario.

On most maps of Canada, Ontario is the big vacuum between Laprairie and Portage la Prairie. Smack in the centre, it is Canada's navel, a collector of lint.

It is where one-third of the country's population naps.

It is governed by a party which has been in power so long it can direct the province in its sleep. And most days it does.

Glance quickly at a map and note how a mere squinting of the eyes and a slight twist of imagination convert the southern portion of the province into an elephant. Note how Windsor marks the curled trunk. Note how St. Catharines marks the leading foot, and how Barrie marks the trailing foot. Note how Tobermory marks the elephant's tail. Note how Owen Sound would rather be somewhere else.

Today not much happens in Ontario. This is about the same as yesterday or a week ago last Thursday. But this is not true for the rest of Canada. And this keeps Ontario occupied.

Tales of adventure on the rugged Maritime coasts are written in Ontario. The true experiences of life on the lonely Prairies are created in Ontario. The anguish of the Quebec's cultural division is recorded in Ontario. The culture of B.C.'s divided anguish is enjoyed in Ontario. Thousands of innocent Atlantic seals have been saved in Ontario. Hundreds of Inuit have had their civilization preserved in Ontario. Dozens of Newfoundlanders have blown their wages in Ontario.

Ontario has no identifiable culture of its own for the very good reason that it has been too busy generously creating everyone else's.

Whatever the rest of Canada thinks of Ontario, Ontario has its own views of the nation. It's just too modest to talk about them.

Quebec, for instance, is regarded fondly as a prime exporter of insurance companies and used English road signs.

Saskatchewan is full of potash. Nobody in Ontario knows what a potash is, except that if Saskatchewan didn't have it, there would be a lot more Saskatchewanites on welfare.

Manitoba is a flat place to drive through to go look at potash.

British Columbia has green hills for climbing in summer, white hills for sliding down in winter, and a lot of weird people, some of them not even elected.

On a map, Prince Edward Island could be mistaken for an offshore yam. New Brunswick is crawling with spruce budworms and K.C. Irving, interchangeably. Nova Scotia is Latin for New Haggis.

Newfoundland is what Farley Mowat writes about from his home in Port Hope, Ontario, and the Yukon is what Pierre Berton writes about from his home in Kleinburg, Ontario. The Northwest Territories are what the bureaucrats write about from their offices in Ottawa.

Alberta is what everybody avoids writing about. Ontario is still sore that Alberta built its oil empire out of a few tons of Depression emergency rations (*see* dried fish) and second-hand cars (*see* clunkers) donated by thoughtful businessmen from Central Canada. If Ontario had known it could have built a fortune on dried fish and old cars, it would have kept them.

This is the foundation of much of our national discontent.

Some Canadians think Ontario has all the zest of cold porridge, but even cold porridge can be nutritious. Ontario's history books have heretofore left out the salt. Too bad. Let's have another go.

The salt shaker, please.

Prologue

At the First Congress of the People's Symbols of the Province of Ontario, the Trillium took the chair. Rapping a maple gavel upon a handy toadstool, the Trillium called the forest to order. Misused and abused by the government of Ontario, the symbols were organizing.

"This Symbols Congress has now begun," she cried, her triumvirate of divine petals shivering and shaking in appreciation of the magnificent moment.

"Point of order," shouted the Blue Jay.

"The chair recognizes the Blue Jay," the Trillium stamened. "What's your point?"

"What gives you the right to be chairman?" the Blue Jay screamed. "I'm an official symbol too. What gives you the right to take over?"

"Well," the Trillium smiled sweetly, "I've been an official symbol a long, long time, You're just a jaybird-come-lately. Without your blue coat, you're nothing. You're just a front for the Conservative party. On the other hand, I am a symbol of all that is pure and hopeful in the forests of Ontario."

"May I speak to the point of order?" the White Pine sighed. The White Pine was always sighing in the winds of change. "It is true that you have been a symbol for a long time, and that the Blue Jay has only recently been elected to the Symbol Congress. But I have been around Ontario for many, many years. My forefathers stood tall on the shores of Huron when the first Blue Jay arrived after spring training in Florida. My ancestors shaded the forest floor where the very first trillium spread her petals to the morning sun. We have been here in Ontario for eons. Surely I should be considered for the chair of the First Congress of the People's Symbols."

The Trillium smirked. "But nobody recognizes you for a symbol. You serve best when you're cut up into little boards. It's not that you're slow, White Pine, but you do seem to spend a lot of your time just lumbering along. I agree, you are good for a chair, but only as one to sit on."

She chortled and chuckled at her joke, and failed to see the Moose and the Bear and the Deer sneaking into the Congress. Suddenly, the Moose was standing directly in front of her. "Me and the Bear and the Deer want to be considered, too. We been on the coat of arms longer than any of youse guys, and we think we qualify as official symbols."

The Congress went dead silent. The Moose and the Bear and the Deer were powerful creatures. Not the Deer alone, perhaps, but she was strong and powerful when backed by the might of the Moose and the Bear.

Outside the Congress Cave, a clamor of forest chaos arose in a chorus. The other creatures of the forest, members of the American Amalgamated Union of Flora and Fauna (Canada), were clamoring for admission.

The Centipede cried, "I wanna be the official insect."

"You're a political liability. Too metric. I wanna be!" squeaked the Termite.

"Oh, you're too boring," sniffed the Ant. "Me, I'm industrious, just like the province."

"You're more like the government," said the Housefly, "always underfoot."

The grumph of the Bullfrog swamped the cacophony. "I should be the official amphibian."

And then the eerie cry of the Common Loon pierced the uproar. "I should have been the official bird. For who resembles politicians more than I? I float with the current, and duck out of sight at the first sign of danger."

Inside the Congress Cave, the Trillium was aware that organization of the official symbols could not be accomplished without agreement on a chairemblem. Suddenly the cavern went stony silent. The Amethyst was rolling towards the Trillium, shrugging off centuries of moss as he trundled along.

"I am the most senior of all," he thundered. "I am the Official Rock of Ontario, and I am more permanent than any of you. All of you are living creatures, and as such you come and you go. I, however, have always been here. And what better symbol of Ontario could you want? You, Trillium, blossom. You, White Pine, sigh and wave about in the wind. You, Blue Jay, make a lot of racket. But I am inanimate. I just sit, and look pretty."

And all the official symbols cheered and clapped and whistled as they unanimously elected the Amethyst chairemblem of the First Congress of the People's Symbols.

PART I

The Age of the Trillium

The trillium bursts forth its glory to signal the birth of another season of verdant growth. Ontario's birth has long been masked by mythology, and only now do we learn the truth about the secret vice of Laura Secord's cow, why a local newspaper welcomed the arrival of the Yanks at Fort York, and how perverse liquor laws were the real cause of the Rebellion of 1837.

West of the Frenchies

· PENNSYLVANIA ·
April, 1784

Martha Kingtoadie was whining again about the shortcomings of her social set. That afternoon at the flagging bee, she had been forced to endure the humiliations of the Flag Mistress.

"If Betsy Ross bugs me one more time," Martha complained, "she'll be wearing her next flag for diapers, permanently pinned in place. You should hear her go on! 'You ain't got the stars in a perfect circle,' she says. 'That third stripe is crooked. Make a wider hem. Ben wouldn't fly that one from a kite string, let alone a flag pole.' If you ask me, the silly bugger wouldn't know the difference."

George Kingtoadie sighed. Before the People's Revolution, his wife had spent much of her time at quilting bees. He had wondered why she abandoned her family to spend time with a bunch of women who, according to her stories, only made her life miserable. But now that the women had switched from stitching quilts to stitching flags, her constant carping had turned bitter.

There was more than just bad blood between Betsy and Martha. Betsy had awarded herself the grandiose title of Daughter of the American Revolution. Martha, in her direct style, had shortened it to "That Bitch."

Although revolting at times, Martha was no daughter of any revolution. She was, like George, not much in favor of booting out the King's men. She liked the Old Order. It wasn't a matter of love of King and Empire and all that rot, but things had been so neat and tidy before old Maple-molar Washington and his ruffians spoiled the system. Before the revolution, it had been a matter of sending off your taxes to the King once in a while, and keeping your nose clean. Now everyone was involved in drafting the militia, drafting legislation, or in her case, drafting new flags.

She went to the flag bees to keep up a pretense of loyalty to the new government. Refusal to attend would have cast suspicion on her family. Besides, she could not resist the neighborhood grapevine. The spies looking for traitors to the revolutionary cause were a prime source of gossip. They hadn't found many traitors when they peeked in people's windows, but they had managed to locate quite a few temporarily wayward spouses.

George personally thought some of the influential members of the governing gang were a bit dotty. Like that fellow Ben Franklin. He didn't even know enough to come in out of the rain. If there was thunder and lightning, he was out flying kites. Not long ago, thought George, a man surviving a lightning strike would have been burned at the stake as a warlock.

Of course, circumstances had driven him to flying kites. The poor beggar went mad as the Postmaster General in Quebec. By the Lord Lilyliver, that post office in Quebec was a warren of unrest. Postal workers only showed up for work to steal their share of beaver skins from the weekly mail to Britain. One winter, a gang of bored posties stole the Trois Rivières post office itself, chopped up the log building, and sold it to the poor for firewood. They were suspended a day for failing to return the axe.

Little wonder that poor Ben had fled Quebec, kite in hand. But George had never understood why he had tried to convince Quebec to join the revolution. Did he really want to import Quebec postal workers to Philadelphia? Why, they'd steal the crack out of the Liberty Bell.

"George," Martha whimpered, "I've had enough of this revolutionary nonsense. For the last eight years, we've heard of nothing else but constitution, constitution, constitution. You'd think those lawyers in Philadelphia had nothing else to do. Every time they think they've got it straightened out, some backwoods state objects and they've got to do it all over again. Conference after conference, court after court. I'm telling you, George, I really miss the good old days when all we had to know were the words to "God Save the King." George wasn't much—not you dear, the King—what with his addled brain and all, but there was something solid about having a monarch. Know what I mean? None of this constitution stuff, and amendments, and reciting the declaration of independence, and knowing which hand to hold over your heart at the baseball games."

George realized that he was not going to be able to conceal his wife's hatred for the revolution much longer. They would have to seek a new homeland.

"Martha, get the children out of bed. We have to talk to them."

"George, have I said something wrong?"

"Not wrong, Martha, just too much. It's all over."

"Oh, George, don't leave me. I'll behave, I promise I will, but please don't leave me."

"Martha, nobody's leaving anybody, but please don't extend the invitation. Get the children."

Martha disappeared into the cabin loft to wake her family. Soon the small Kingtoadie brood was assembled in front of George: Alphonse, 15, Bettina, 14, Calvin, 13, Delphinia, 12, Ebenezer, 11, Faustina, 10, Gardiner, 9, Heloise, 8, Ignatius, 7, Jessica, 6, Kevin, 5, Lavinia, 4, Montgomery, 3, Nettie, 2, and Osbert, 1.

"Children," began George.

"Father," replied the sleepy children's chorus.

"Children, your mother has driven me to decide ... I mean, your mother and I have decided that we would really rather not live in this neighborhood any more."

"Oh, good," said Alphonse. "Can I have your room?"

"Dummy, you always want the best," cried Bettina. "Father, give it to Delphinia and me." Several other children set up a clamor to claim the coveted master bedroom.

"No, you don't understand," said George. "We're all going to move. Your mother and I are not entirely in agreement with the ideas of some of our neighbors, and we think that we would be happier if we moved elsewhere." He had to be extremely careful not to say anything disparaging about the Revolutionary Government, lest one of the younger children repeat it at Show and Tell next day.

"Uh, Father, does that mean we're going to become Loyalists?" asked Ebenezer.

"It does," said his father.

There was a long silence. Ebenezer finally spoke. "You wouldn't be thinking of following the others, would you?"

George steeled himself. Sometimes a wise father had to dish out cruel and unusual punishment for the good of his family. They would hate him now but thank him in the years ahead.

He swept his gaze slowly over them, looking deeply into their souls. They stared stonily back. He thought he detected a few sneers at his weak behavior. He took a deep breath, then said, "Please, children, remember that your father loves you."

All of the children, even infant Osbert, seemed to stiffen with dread anticipation. George plunged on. There was no way he could delay the inevitable discussion.

"Yes, we're going to Canada."

When the Kingtoadie children calmed down, they resorted to their polite form of speaking in order.

"Arctic," sobbed Alphonse.

"Blackflies," sneered Bettina.

"C-c-c-cold," coughed Calvin.

"Deep freeze," chortled Delphinia.

"Eskimos," exclaimed Ebenezer.

"Frogs," shouted Faustina.

"Glaciers," cried Gardiner.

"Horsemeat," wept Heloise.

"Icebergs," whooped Ignatius.

"Jesuits," giggled Jessica.

"Kanata," peeped Kevin.

"Lost," laughed Lavinia.

"Maple surple," burbled Montgomery.

Nettie and Osbert, handicapped with an inadequate vocabulary at their tender years, conveyed their feelings in less conventional fashions. Nettie threw up and Osbert dirtied his diaper.

Martha glared red-hot anger. "George, I don't know what we'll do up there. You know if there's one food I detest more than maple syrup, it's tourtière. I mean, I know it keeps those Frenchmen alive, but I don't know how. Why in heaven's name did we English let those Frenchmen stay on anyway. I'd have shipped them all back to France. They're going to cause trouble."

George tried to ignore her. He didn't have to glance her way to know that her neck was as red as the cross of St. George. Martha whined on, "Oh sure, they're tame now. The King lets them *parlez-vous* around, doing whatever they like, and everybody's happy. But you mark my words, there's trouble ahead."

George closed his eyes. "Not now, Martha. Not in front of the children."

"Well, they might as well know all about this great new land you've chosen for them. Those frogs are going to cause problems. They breed, you know. It's in their church. They'll breed like crazy and before we know it, they'll demand to be serviced in their own language. Our young ones, if they all live to grow up in that harsh world you've picked out, won't be able to get a job with the government unless they speak French. And where are they going to learn that? Are you going to get a second job in a grist mill so we can hire a tutor?"

George reconsidered his promise not to leave her, then thought the better of it. They would all go to Canada. He'd convince them it was a good idea somehow, although he'd rather sell iceboxes to Eskimos. He winced as he realized he might need to moonlight as an icebox salesman.

Alphonse began needling his mother. "Hey, Mom, did you know they only have two seasons in Canada? Winter and July 20." The other children giggled; Martha wailed.

"Mom," Alphonse was at it again, "Mom, they've got a game called hockey up there. They play it on ice. You'll love it. Only problem is, the only good hockey they've got is in the land of the Frenchies. My witchcraft teacher says it has something to do with natural rhythm."

Martha burst into tears. George moved in quickly. "Listen, we're not going to any land of the Frenchies. There's a lot of good land west of the Frenchies—I mean, west of Montreal—where we'll be welcomed by our own kind. If we get enough of us up there, we can ask the King to give us our own government. He's mad as a wet toad at the frogs for siding with the revolutionaries, so he'll understand. Besides, he hates pea soup. He can't suck it through a straw."

"Father, why can't we just stay here and be good American citizens?" asked Calvin. "I know it's tough for you and Mother to learn the new system, but in a generation we'll all be converted. We're all learning republican at school now. When Nettie and Osbert grow up, they won't even be aware that a monarchy ever existed. They'll measure everything in republican terms. It would be a lot easier than moving to a place where you've got one day a year to grow your crops."

George stammered, "Oh, come on. Alphonse was only teasing about the one-day summer. It's longer than that. Some years it lasts most of a month, although they can never be sure which month."

He was staggered. His very own children had been brainwashed. They believed in republicanism. While he had been tilling the fields and Martha had been slaving at the flagshop, his own flesh and blood had been transformed into allies of the new republic. Madly, he searched his mind for another compelling argument.

"Look, if we become Canadians, everyone in the world will love us, if they think of us. You won't have to carry a gun to get respect. Wherever there's a war, we'll be invited in to make peace. If our army has a gun, we'll bring it along without the bullet. You'll be able to travel anywhere in the world with pride and confidence in being a Canadian. You will be free to walk into any gift shop, declare your Canadian citizenship, and proudly pay another 20 cents on the dollar. People will welcome you everywhere and say, 'Thank God you're not a Yank,' and then start talking about American politics. You'll be a citizen of the world, embraced by all and indebted to none."

The children, a dreamy look in their eyes, began to hum "God Save the King." Martha bit her lip and brushed away a tear. George could not continue speaking, so large was the lump in his throat.

Finally, Alphonse, the eldest child, addressed his father. "Gee, it sounds great. But will we ever be able to come back here?"

George smiled. "Of course. After a while, up in Canada we'll be treated like just another state of the union."

First Throne Speech Assembly of Upper Canada

~1792~

Governor Simcoe: Ladies and gentlemen, honored guests, and representatives to the first assembly of the new, or should I say, recently unattached, that is not to say divorced, region of Upper Canada, this is a beautiful day in the development of our nation as it is, I am sure, just as beautiful in downtown Brampton, and I am sure it is equally beautiful in our sister province of Lower Canada which is still primarily in the hands of those of the French persuasion

who, I am given to understand, extend to us assembled here the best wishes they could summon under the circumstances, given the constraints imposed upon them by the Roman Catholic Church, which is not a bad church necessarily nor is it a particularly good church but it is a church for all intents and purposes which

nevertheless by trying to keep its parishioners happy and content extends to us its wishes for having a successful start on this, and I say this from the bottom of my heart, glorious day here in Upper Canada, and I wish to echo those sentiments exactly, I think, as does my wife Elizabeth who never makes speeches but shares my emotions and thoughts from time to time although I'm never sure whether it's on my time or on hers—ho, ho, ho—but I am sure that on this glorious day she would be willing to support my good wishes whole, or should I say at least half, heartedly.

As we commence to start our beginning towards and into the development, and I don't use that word lightly, of a great football team which shall be called the Toronto Argonauts and, incidentally, our new province and I say new in the sense that it was not here yesterday except as an adjunct of our sister province to the east, and I don't use the word 'east' pejoratively—well, listen, I don't, I never have and I never will—this development which will one day include the Great City of Brampton ... there, that's twice I've mentioned it ... this development has its beginnings in today and its roots in yesterday and all that we shall accomplish, and I am confident that we shall accomplish much ..."

An Hon. Member: "As soon as you finish this sentence."

Governor Simcoe: "The honorable member obviously is not interested in progress, peace, and prosperity. Well, I am, as soon as I finish these few introductory remarks which in their brevity are the antithesis of ..."

An Hon. Member: "Auntie Who?"

Governor Simcoe: "What's that? ... well, you can look it up later ... the antithesis of the great and glorious future of this Great Province of Upper Canada which, although it has not yet become a household word in the courts of Europe, and I realize that the courts of Europe have many important issues on their minds, will someday occupy the forefront of the background of the middle ground that we are only now beginning to start to commence. Thank you.

Where Numbers Warrant

The sun was sinking low over the westward hills and a cool evening breeze rustled the leaves along the shores of Penetanguishene Bay. Colonel Davis Williams propped his boot-clad feet up on his desk and silently thanked his superiors for his new posting.

Fort Penetanguishene wasn't exactly Oxford, but it wasn't Quebec City either. And now Quebec City would be only a stopover on his way home to England after this tour of duty. The worst part of Quebec City was that the British could not fully enjoy their role as conquerors.

Col. Williams winced. He'd tried to anglicize the French, but his commander always rebuffed him.

Orders were orders. The King, on advice from pompous liberal layabouts in his court, had decided that the French could be better controlled if they were allowed to keep their own language, religion, and culture. History would look kindly on a generous British conqueror, and the French would have no cause for complaint.

But here in the wilderness, Col. Davis Williams was in charge. He

had control. First thing he'd do, he'd shorten the name. Penetang. Fort Penetanguishene cluttered up the road signs.

A light knocking at the door broke into his thoughts. Corporal Ralph Holland shambled in. "There's someone demanding to see you, sir. It's the parish priest, François de L'eau-Perrier. He wants to see you about the French school."

Col. Williams stared at him. There were still quite a few things to learn about Fort Penetanguishene, he realized. He had only been here four days. But surely Cpl. Holland could have told him about the school.

"Cpl. Holland, just what is wrong with the school?"

"What's wrong, sir? Nothing, except that there isn't one."

"Oh. Should there be? What's wrong with the English school?"

"Nothing, sir. It's perfectly sturdy. It's well equipped. But it's the law, sir."

Col. Williams hesitated, then realized he couldn't conceal his ignorance. "Okay, corporal, what law are we talking about?"

"The numbers law, sir. Under the British Conqueror's Fair Play to Froggies Act, 1765, minority language education must be provided in areas where numbers warrant. Father L'eau-Perrier says his numbers warrant."

Col. Williams exploded. "Bloody 'ell! What numbers? Whose numbers? I'll bet he's responsible for half of them. How come the numbers are suddenly warranting this week when

I'm commander, and they weren't last week when old Sneadly was in charge?"

Cpl. Holland shuffled his feet. "Well, sir, I beg your pardon, but it's because of your arrival."

Col. Williams thought he might just be about to have a heart attack here on the shores of Penetanguishene Bay, but he managed to croak out, "Explain yourself, corporal, unless you want a three-year diet of tourtière in Quebec."

"Well, sir, you arrived with a French bearer. You brought him along, you said, as your butler. He brought his family which, you'll recall, includes two children. That was enough to raise the local student population over the 'numbers warrant' quota."

"And this means?"

"This means you must build the French school."

In his mind's eye, Col. Williams bent himself double and booted himself severely in the backside. He'd forgotten all about that silly law. In Quebec there were so many frogs around it never had to be used. Everything was provided automatically. The worst of it was, he had hired the French bearer because he was half-a-guinea cheaper than an Englishman.

"Corporal, show in Father Loop-Holer."

"It's L'eau-Perrier."

"Whatever. Let's get on with it."

Father L'eau-Perrier was a naturally bubbly little chap, not pretentious and certainly satisfying in the confessional. He rushed across the room to greet Col. Williams. *'Ah, mon ami nouveau, le colonel. Quel plaisir de vous recontre. C'est une grande occasion. J'ai ..."*

Col. Williams interrupted. "Welcome, father. We must speak in English, for I don't know your language at all."

Father L'eau-Perrier frowned for a moment, then smiled. "Okay, buddy, if that's the way you want it. Be a *maudit anglais,* for all I care. Frankly, I'd rather use English too, because I was raised in London. My father was in debtor's prison, and for that I became a child slave to the Earl of Boringthumberlancastershire. But I ran off when I was twelve. Showed up the old bugger, and believe me, he was that. I stowed away in a ship, wound up working for nothing for a French crew for five years, and finally escaped in Quebec. By that time I could speak fluent French, but I was afraid I'd be found out by the British authorities there, so I made my way by Coureurs-de-bois Express to this wretched hole. I'm tired of running, colonel. Put the cuffs on me and send me back. Got any beer?"

Col. Williams snarled, "No. Now what kind of cheap trick is this? I thought you wanted a French school."

"Oh, I don't give a damn about the school. What I really care about is getting back to England without going back to the earl, that fat turkey. Of course, if you can't arrange it, I'll have to have my school."

The colonel was aghast. "You're talking about blackmail."

Father L'eau-Perrier grinned. "I should have known the British army wouldn't entrust Fort Penetanguishene to a dummy. Ah, colonel, you've seen right through my plan. Careless of me, I guess."

Col. Williams sputtered, "I won't have anything to do with a Frenchman, or worse, an Englishman masquerading as a Frenchman, blackmailing an officer of the Crown."

Father L'eau-Perrier opened a cupboard door and peered inside. "Any whiskey? No? Okay. I don't go back to England. You write to Quebec City for money to build a French school that wasn't needed last week. You explain how you exploited the French bearer and brought two French children here to put the numbers over the 'warranted' quota. Go ahead. The Frenchies here will love it. It strikes one more blow for their culture. They don't need the school any more than I do, but they'll take what they can from the English."

Col. Williams slumped in his chair. "And if I do neither?"

"Ah, mon colonel, maintenant vous etes très stupide. If you do not give me a French school, then I shall have to write Quebec City. I shall complain about how you exploit the French, and I shall complain about how you are failing to provide a French school as required by law. I shall do all this as Father L'eau-Perrier, of course. That will carry a lot of weight in Quebec City. I expect

the Government will send out a commission to investigate and when it gets here, I shall have no choice but to demonstrate, however sadly, that the poor misguided British colonel obviously is not sensitive enough to govern a minority group."

Col. Williams grimaced. There was no choice. He could not afford to be given a bad name in Quebec.

"And you may get home to England sooner than you thought," continued Father L'eau-Perrier, "but without your rank. Or maybe, you will get another three-year indoctrination course in Quebec City. Me, I can live here forever, but I'd rather

not. Now, which of us goes back to England first?"

The colonel slouched. "All right, you do. I shall have to hire you as personal staff and send you home as my agent on urgent personal business. And when you get home, I want you to deliver a letter."

Father L'eau-Perrier looked puzzled. "A letter? To who?"

"To whom, you lout. To my father, the earl of Boringthumberlancastershire. I want him to kick your butt every day before breakfast and twice on Sundays until I return, then I'll take over when I inherit the title. It'll be such a pleasure, Father Loop-Holer."

Even Eve Wore a Leaf

· YORK ·

June 14, 1794

Gov. John Graves Simcoe paused at the door to his tent, drew his sword, took a deep breath and prepared to plunge into his canvas home in the Canadian wilderness. Elizabeth was inside, having tea with Tom Talbot, his personal secretary. In these last few weeks, he had never entered his own home without first drawing his sword.

Not because of Talbot. He understood perfectly well the arrangement and understanding between his wife and his secretary. Talbot had introduced her to the wilds of Canada, and she had fallen in love. Not with Talbot, but with flora and fauna, not to mention flowers and fawns, and all kinds of creepy little critters that no sane English gardener would tolerate in the hedgerows of home.

The trouble was, Elizabeth wanted to bring them all home to their tent in York. There were three kazillion square miles of Canada, and she wanted all her friends sharing her bedroll. (Not Talbot. Her friends from the forest.) Lately, he had discovered she was no longer content with Canadian greenery. A dozen imported plants in hanging baskets had arrived from the Orient that very morning.

Simcoe cautiously raised the flap of his tent. He leaped back as a tendril of lipstick vine (*aeschynanthus lobbianus*) shot towards him through the opening. He swung his sword wildly, hacking off three feet of vine and barely missing his own two.

"Elizabeth!" he roared. A nerve plant (*fittonia vershaffeltii*), cowering at the doorsill, shivered and scurried back inside the tent.

Enough of this nonsense. Simcoe pulled aside the tent flap and pushed his way inside. A gardenia jasminoides scuttled into the corner. Creeping Jennie (*lysimachia nummularie*), poised on a tent pole, threw herself at Simcoe's cocked hat. With a flourish of his sword, he cut poor Jennie off at the roots.

"Elizabeth!" he shouted again. "Come out of that damn jungle!"

Beyond the impenetrable foliage, in the steamy mists at the rear of the tent, there was a sudden rattling of teacups. A rattling too frantic by half, thought Simcoe. There was possibly the rustling of an evergreen mattress too, but he couldn't be sure. It might just have been the breeze sighing through the spider plants (*chlorophytum comosum*).

"Coming, dear!" cried Elizabeth. "Tom and I were just having tea. Would you care for some? It's delightful. Lamb's quarters and sumach leaf."

"No, thanks. Elizabeth, how do you expect me to run a command post for Upper Canada out of this fernery? Just yesterday, I got a letter back from Lord Dorchester, who complained that I had pressed maple leaves in the annual military report from Fort Niagara. He thought it was a poignant touch, but wondered if the wilderness was getting to me. How am I supposed to explain that kind of thing to England?"

Talbot, ducking his way around the dangling strawberry geraniums (*saxafraga stolonifera*), came to Elizabeth's aid. "Sir, I'll take the blame for the maple leaves. I thought a whimsical touch would tell them back home that all was well in Upper Canada. If the commander has time to press colored leaves, surely he can't be worried about the Yanks."

"Thanks, Col. Talbot. Next time, send the report without the maple leaves. Has anyone seen my desk?"

"It's over there, behind the Boston fern." Elizabeth pointed frondly to a dense growth of *nephrolepis exaltata*.

"All right, all right, that does it." Simcoe's face reddened. "I don't mind you importing all these precocious salad ingredients from Asia and Africa and beyond, even from Kapuskasing, but nothing from Boston. And not in front of my desk. What IS that on my desk?"

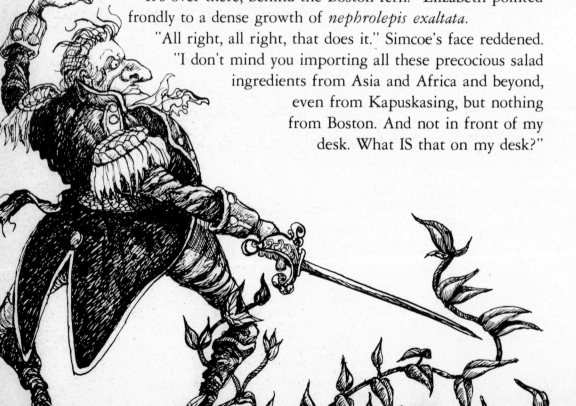

Talbot said, "It's a terrarium, sir. Certain plants and animals grow best under glass. This way, we can keep the rattlesnakes out of your bedclothes."

Simcoe's hand flew to the hilt of his sword. "Rattlesnakes? Where? In this tent?"

Elizabeth, as smooth as ever, took Simcoe by the arm. "They're not so bad, once you get to know them. I've even named one of them Dorchester, after your boss. He hisses a lot, but he broke his fangs on a bottle."

Now pale and shaking, Simcoe said, "Elizabeth, I am going to go for a ride to inspect the Queen's Rangers. I shall be back at sunset, at which time I shall expect this tent to be rid of spiders, both plants and creepy crawlers, ferns, vines, and those ugly rattlesnakes. Let them go, Elizabeth. If you must have them around, why not become an artist and paint them?"

Simcoe strode through the tent flap, angrily brushing back a Chinese hibiscus (*hibiscus rosa-sinensis*) and tripping over a Mother-in-law plant (*dieffenbachia*).

As the hoofbeats of his horse slowly faded in the distance, Elizabeth turned to Talbot. "Well, dear, an order is an order. Your commander and my husband has spoken. But you know, it would be a shame to waste all these plants. When I was walking along the beaches east of here last week, I was thinking that area deserves a leafy restaurant. Bring the outdoors inside, I thought. That *would* be trendy, don't you think?"

Back of Bancroft
· FORT NIAGARA ·
June, 1811

What I remember most about that day in the back of Hagerman's General Store was the heat. We were only a small town council, seven I think, but when we pushed ourselves into a tiny storeroom with the nail kegs and the hatchets and the bales of canvas, things really got hot. And of course, we were nervous.

This was an emergency town council meeting. It was so hush-hush that even Hagerman's wife didn't know we were there. What a burden for him! She was the biggest gossip in town—she came from Boston—and here he was, trying to conduct a secret session in his own storeroom.

See, we were meeting about the foreigners in our midst. There was a war coming on. We knew it, they knew it, and we didn't know what they'd do when it happened. Y'see, most of us had come straight to Upper Canada from the Motherland. Britain, I mean. *They* had come from the United States.

Oh, we knew they called themselves Loyalists and promised to be faithful to the King. But we also knew most of them had friends and family back in Pennsylvania and New England. Some had friends right across the river in New York. We didn't really know where their loyalties would lie if push came to shove. Besides that, they were a bunch of bloody mercenaries who would sell their grandmothers for a barrel of whiskey.

So we called a meeting of council, because Larry Kelston had an idea that he said made sense to him, which didn't necessarily mean it would make sense to the rest of us. Sometimes Kelston took a strange approach to life.

We had just started our meeting in the storeroom when we were reminded why we were there. I mean, we knew why we were there, but a reminder walked into Hagerman's General Store and we had to be quiet and pretend we weren't there. Hagerman had to go out front and look after the customer.

It was George Appleton. Now, ordinarily, we liked Appleton. He was about 48, a rough-looking man, but he was a decent and honest fellow who contributed his share to the community. He was a farmer, and he and his wife had emigrated to Upper Canada from the Albany area of New York back in '84. But, y'see, that was the problem. He still had two brothers back in the States, and all of his wife's family, and they got a lot of mail from down that way.

Hagerman's was also the post office, and Appleton used to open his mail right in the store, after the stage came through. Not through the store, you understand, but through town. He delighted in reading aloud his brothers' descriptions of prosperity in the United States, and he'd go on and on about how maybe he had made a mistake, and maybe we'd all be better off if we joined the United States. Then he'd roar with laughter and say he'd made his bed so he'd have to lie in it.

We were never quite sure about him.

Now the point is, there were a lot of people around us like Appleton. And we were afraid that if war broke out with the Americans, we'd have sympathizers in our midst. That was what our meeting was about. And, by golly, when Kelston outlined his idea, it wasn't half bad at that.

What he said was that we all liked these people. We agreed. He said we didn't want to do them any harm. We agreed again. But, he said, we couldn't trust them if a war came. We agreed whole-heartedly.

"So," said Kelston, "why don't we just move them back into the bush for a while until this blows over? We'd have to get them away from the Great Lakes and Georgian Bay, of course, because they might be able to help the American navy." So he suggested we contact General Isaac Brock, our temporary government administrator, and have the Loyalists shifted back-country.

I saw one immediate problem, and I said so. I said Brock would not tolerate any deprivation of private property. Kelston said nobody would lose any property. The government would hold onto their land until after the war. If the Americans happened to win, the Loyalists would appear to have been prisoners of war and would easily get their land back. If we won, why, we'd give the land back, probably with the crops already planted and chickens laying eggs in the henhouse.

The positive side, he said, was that the Loyalists would open up new land in the back country. In the long run, Upper Canada would be expanded and become all the more prosperous. During the war they could farm back there around Peterborough and Bancroft, and nobody would bother them.

Well, it seemed like a reasonable plan to all of us. The only drawback was that there were about four Loyalists to every one of us, and we couldn't figure out how we could make them understand why this was necessary.

We took the plan to General Brock anyway, and the rest is history. He didn't move all the Loyalists, but he took the ones from around the sensitive military areas like Fort George and Fort York. That's how they wound up with all that rich farmland between Madoc and Bancroft. Unfortunately, the government felt compelled to sell their lands at York and Niagara to raise money to fight the war. People like Hagerman and Kelston and myself, well, as loyal supporters of the King, we felt compelled to buy the land and that's how we wound up with our estates. But that's another story.

The Wines of Grimsby

"Where the hell is that damned cow?"

Laura Secord was not given to using this sort of language in polite
company in the kitchen, or even among polite cows in the stable. In the
stable it curdled the milk; in the kitchen, the chocolates. But whenever she
had been pursuing old Grimsby through the bush for three hours without
success, she was sometimes apt to draw on a secret mental dictionary.

Grimsby had a habit of wandering off. She always came home on her
own a day or so later, but she never walked quite right. Stumbled, she did,
and lurched around bumping into things. Her milk was a bit off too, and
her eyes had an unusually glassy look.

Laura was mystified. "It's just as if she were drunk," she said to her
candy-cooking class one night, "but I know cows don't drink."

And now, Grimsby had slunk off again into the bush. In normal
times, Laura would have let her come
home whenever, but these weren't
normal times. American soldiers were
about, trespassing on the soil of

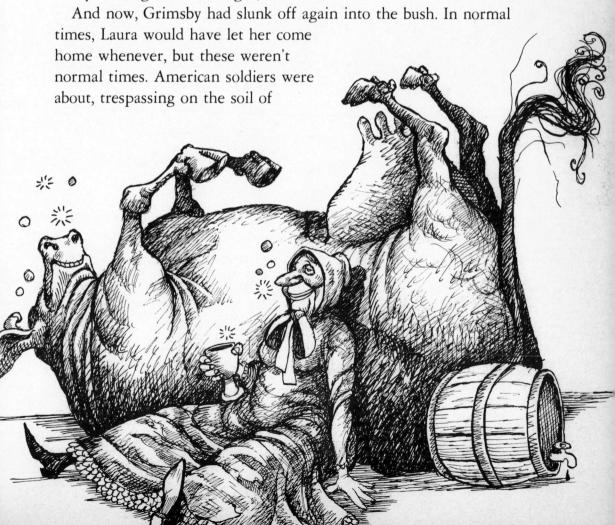

Upper Canada, and they would just as soon take the steaks from a stray cow as the milk. Laura shivered. She hoped she wouldn't meet any soldiers on the path. They weren't always gentlemen.

"Grimsby!" she called. "Grimsby! Here bossy, here bossy!"

Laura pushed on until she came to a clearing in the bush. It wasn't a natural opening. It was a man-made patch, an evenly-cut square of cultivation smack in the middle of a hardwood forest. It was not marked on the settlers' charts. The field was about 100 acres in size, which in today's metric terms is about 34 cubic litres, or 15 kilopascals measured diagonally.

The field was not empty. There were rows and rows of grapevines, propped up on stakes. A rough little log cabin stood in the middle, and wooden barrels of various sizes lay scattered about.

Laura took a closer look. The top of one of the barrels had been knocked off, and was laying beside it on the ground. There was more than the lid laying on the ground. There was Grimsby laying on the ground, all eight undercarriage protuberances (four hooves, four teats) pointing skyward. Grimsby was snoring.

Laura saw that the barrel was half full of some liquid. She dipped in a dainty finger and tasted it. She instantly realized that she had been wrong: the barrel was not half full, it was half empty, and she knew where the other half had gone.

Into Grimsby.

Laura Secord had the world's most contented cow.

"Cor blimey, it's a bloody piece of fluff!" The voice drawled out of the shadows within the cabin. Laura gasped. Had she stumbled into an American trap? Unusual choice of language for a Yank, to be sure. But the form that staggered out of the cabin wore a distinct, if wrinkled, British regular army uniform. "I say, are you looking for something?" the soldier demanded.

"Uh, yes, my cow," said Laura. "It's right there, with its feet in the air."

"Is that your cow? Well, me and the boys wish you would keep it at home. It's ruining our production."

Five other lads, giggling and laughing, stumbled out of the cabin. Some of them lurched more than others, and none walked with ease. "See, mum, we've got something going here that nobody else knows about. We're making wine, mum, and we think we can make a go of it after this war's over, providing we can keep the cows from drinking it all."

Laura was more than a little nervous. The boys were giving her a friendly eyeballing. "You may think we're a little drunk, mum, and maybe we are. But this here is our research station and these here are my researchers. We do this in our spare time. 'Course, we picked this place way back here on purpose, so nobody would find it. But you have, so now we have to talk about this. Would you like a sample?"

Laura accepted. It might make her less nervous and give her a chance to think.

"Now, this is a tasty little red we've created. It's dry, and has good body, but it's just a little strong on the throat. Matter of fact, we've been using it to clean our gun barrels."

Laura took a sip, then quickly spat it out. Onto Grimsby. The cow moaned once, but didn't move.

"This one is less robust, if you like, but it lacks a little color. It appears to be a rosé but it's supposed to be a red. I think we added too much water. Here's one that Zeb over there likes. It's almost purple. See, it clings to the side of the glass, and it certainly has lots of body. The only problem is, you can't drink it unless you hold your nose. We're having a little trouble with the odor. Zeb has a constant case of hay fever, so he doesn't know the difference."

Laura peered into another barrel. "Ma'am," said the chief researcher, "you certainly have an eye for quality. That there barrel holds our best product. Here, try a glass." Laura did. The third mouthful hardly burned at all. She took another swallow. The chief researcher droned on, while Laura emptied her glass and drew another from the barrel. These boys weren't so bad. Besides, she couldn't go home until Grimsby revived.

Glass of wine followed glass of wine, and what happened in the next few hours is best left for another story. Laura was not at all accustomed to the new wines of Niagara.

Grimsby eventually did come around, as did Laura and the researchers. Then the sober truth dawned on them all: poor Laura had spent all night in the unchaperoned company of several young and lustful British soldiers.

Sorrow and regret set in. How was Laura to explain her lengthy absence? Could she reasonably expect intelligent friends and neighbors to believe that she had searched all night for a cow and had come home with a gigantic hangover.

No, that would never do. Nobody would believe it. She could say Americans kidnapped her. No, then she'd need a story about escaping. It seemed hopeless.

"I've got it," said the chief researcher. "We don't want anybody tramping around in here looking for Americans, because they might find our vineyard. So what you do is, you tell your family that you heard the Americans were in the neighborhood. You wanted to warn us, so you pretended to be leading your cow through the bush. You got past the Americans, you warned us, and we went out and chased all the big bad Americans away and now you're a hero."

Laura blushed. "Who's going to believe that?"

"It's such a whopper everybody will. This country is ripe for a hero. You can advance the cause of feminism by a century."

Laura sighed. "I'll give it a try. But I won't promise that they won't come looking and find your vineyard."

"Just do your best. You might even write a book and go on tour. It sure beats making candies in the kitchen—there's no fame in that."

How D'ya Like York
So Far?

· YORK, UPPER CANADA ·
April 27, 1813

Fred hated the night shift at the York *Daily Metro Sunstar*. Little enough happened during the day in this burg on Lake Ontario. At night there was nothing better to do than read the foreign news dispatches on the incoming pigeons.

His rare assignments usually involved boring old men arguing boring old points of idiocy. On this night, for instance, he had been sent to the Allbalmy Club to cover a debate on the likelihood of York becoming involved in the current war with the Americans.

Some gentlemen claimed that an attack on York was inevitable because the town was the capital of Upper Canada. A capital was a symbol, and in wartime a good commander always went after symbols. It was a matter of good form, good sportsmanship, and good headlines in the press at home.

Other gentlemen pointed out that no American commander worth his weight in cannonballs would bother coming across Lake Ontario to ravage a tiny village of 600. They'd pursue the military command centres.

As dawn approached, Fred quilled the last of this dreary trash. It hadn't much hope of seeing print, because the York *Daily Metro Sunstar* didn't like to depress people. But old Frank, the night editor, would have a chuckle before he spiked it. Fred turned it in and began to think of heading home.

Frank grunted his appreciation, then said, "You better get down to the beach near the fort. Somebody says there are a bunch of sailing ships offshore, and they ain't fishing boats. Take an artist with you for a quick sketch and if it's anything important, make sure you file something for the first edition."

Fred, grumbling, scrambled around for a piece of parchment and a sharpened quill. As he headed out the door, he yelled at Frank to start recording the overtime. Frank said he would, same as always, which meant he'd buy Fred a beer at Montgomery's, maybe.

When Fred reached the beach a faint glow of dawn—in the east as usual—was tinging the calm waters of Lake Ontario. But even in that dim light, he could make out the black hulks and towering masts of thirteen sailing ships. As the light strengthened, he strained his eyes to identify the bits of rag flapping at the ships' sterns. Eventually, the truth dawned upon Fred as quickly as did the day. Each ship was flying a ragged Betsy Ross.

Fred's heart began to pound. Americans! Here in York! There was no one else around. Blodgett of the *Colonial Mail and Dynasty* was nowhere in sight. This was Fred's big chance, but what he knew about the war was sketchy. He had better not pretend to be a war correspondent. He'd use the "fallback" interview, the one that worked on every visiting foreign celebrity.

A longboat was launched from the nearest ship. Several grubby crewmen clambered into it, then after a slight delay another man in splendid costume leapt in. This was

Fred's target. He watched as the longboat plowed towards shore.

Fred ran down the beach to intercept the longboat. As it ground into the sand and the man in splendid costume stepped out, Fred said eagerly, "Hi, I'm Fred Filcher of the York *Daily Metro Sunstar*. You the commander?"

Splendid Costume eyed him cautiously. "I am," he bragged. "Reynolds Reagan McQueen Bronson Wayne III at your service. Folks just call me Wayne, and that's all right with me. If you call me Queenie I'll knock yer block off. What can I do fer ya?"

Slapping on his readily available "Welcome-to-York" smile, Fred rushed into his Standard Fallback Interview for Foreign Celebrities. "How do you like York so far, Commander Wayne?"

The American squinted at Fred as if the reporter were slightly daft. "Oh, well, seems all right." (Fred wrote, *"Yank says York great city!"*)

"What are you going to see first?" he asked.

"The commander peered around at his crewmen, winked, and turned back to Fred. "Well, I thought I might take a look at your fort." (Fred noted, *"American military leader gets charge from exploring Canadian batteries."*)

"What do you think of our harbor?"

"Wayne glanced up and down the beach and could see nothing but sand, swamp, and Canada geese. "Well, I guess I'd say it has some potential." (Fred scribbled, *"Top American admiral says York port could be world-class."*)

Fred was on a roll. "Have you always wanted to visit York?"

The American paused, thought carefully, and replied. "Nope, can't say as I have." (Fred jotted down, *"York destination spot for crazy impetuous fling."*)

Fred asked, "What inspired you to come?"

Wayne replied, "Oh, you know how it is. Some people come to town, you get to talking, and first thing you know, you want to go travelling." (Fred wrote, *"Everybody's talking about York."*)

"Who came to town?" Fred asked.

"Well, uh, some Brits. They looked us up in Washington with a burning desire to do the town right." (Fred wrote, *"British consumed with fiery passion to see Washington."*) Wayne continued, "When they left, we knew we'd just love to come to York." (Fred wrote, *"British connection draws Yanks to York heart-throb."*)

"What do you think of our tourist facilities?"

The American squinted again. Was this guy for real? As far as he could see, eastward and westward along the shore, hardwoods and evergreens crowded the shoreline of Lake Ontario. A tiny log fort, with its pathetic Union Jack dangling limply from a warped spruce pole, broke the solid wall of green. A few holes in the bush indicated that there might be life in forest clearings. Wayne grunted. "Well, I can't see much from this level." (Fred joyfully quilled, "*Tall free-standing tower would promote York tourism.*")

"Will you be doing much shopping?"

The American snickered. "We didn't bring any money because we don't expect to pay for anything. (Fred wrote, "*American tourists say best of York is free!*")

"Would you like to visit other cities around York?"

The American grinned. "Nope. There's enough to keep me busy right here." (Fred scratched. "*York major tourist magnet of Upper Canada.*")

"One more question. How long will you be staying?"

Wayne shrugged. "Oh, I dunno. The boys would like to get back but we're going to hang onto this place for a few days." (Fred wrote, "*Crew homesick but holidaying American commander can't tear self from York.*")

Fred thanked him, then sprinted back up the beach towards the *Daily Metro Sunstar*. He shouted at the artist, who had wandered off into the bush in search of more birch bark to sketch on. They had a deadline to meet.

On the way back, they met Blodgett of the *Mail and Dynasty* scurrying down towards the waterfront. "Where ya going?" cried Blodgett. "The Americans are attacking the fort!" He hurried on.

Fred chuckled. It was just like Blodgett to work on a war angle and miss the real story. Attacking the fort, indeed. (Fred wrote, "*Frantic foreign fort fans besiege box office for tour tickets.*")

Rule of Thumb

At the second meeting of the Claw Society of Upper Canada, some stringent rules were established to protect the reputations of the members.

A couple of years ago a transcript of that meeting, misfiled between "habeas corpus" and "notwithstanding," was discovered in a basement filing cabinet of Osgoode Hall. It went like this:

Mr. Percival: "Gentlemen, at our first meeting last month we passed only one motion. That order has been carried out and I wish to inform you that the new lock on the door is working magnificently."

Mr. Rumpskull: "Good. There's no point starting a new secret society with an old lock."

Mr. Percival: "Quite. Now then, Mr. Secretary, take down all the names of those present tonight."

Mr. Cornswobble: "I already have."

Mr. Percival: "Thank you. Now burn it. We don't want any records of attendance."

Mr. Cornswobble: "Right."

Mr. Percival: "Now, gentlemen, we have to set up some rules of conduct. First of all, what do we do when one of us gets caught dipping into an old widow's trust fund?"

Mr. Carlisle: "We all share it."

Mr. Percival: "No, no, let's assume that we've been caught red-handed."

Mr. Dumphries: "Are we dipping with fingers? Are we talking single-digit figures? Or are we looking for a rule of thumb? I say we play it safe. We promise that the Society will deal with it."

Mr. Percival: "That's better. Now, how do we deal with it?"

Mr. Dumphries: "We put the complaint in that round file in the floor and buy the old widow's mortgage for a pittance. Then a year later, we put out a news release with a lot of words blacked out, and say that the terrible sot who did this nasty deed has been reprimanded by the Society."

Mr. Percival: "Nice, nice. I like it. How do we reprimand this terrible sot?"

Mr. Carlisle: "We demand shares of his take."

Mr. Percival: "Good, good. Now, what do we do if someone complains that we overcharged him?"

Mr. Didlittle: "Sent him another bill and charge for the extra paper and postage."

Mr. Percival: "What if he persists?"

Mr. Dumphries: "We promise that the Society will deal with it."

Mr. Percival: "And how do we deal with it?"

Mr. Dumphries: "We wait a year, and put out a news release with a lot of words blacked out, and say that the terrible sot who did this nasty deed has been reprimanded by the Society."

Mr. Percival: "What about the fellow who complained?"

Mr. Dumphries: "He goes on our black list. Nobody handles his accounts again. Ever."

Mr. Percival: "Fine, fine. Now, we have to do something about keeping up with the doctors."

Mr. Ledger: "No problem. Every time they issue a new fee schedule, we add 30 per cent to ours and demand equal tee-off time."

Mr. Percival: "That covers the basics. Gentlemen, let's adjourn. And don't forget: nobody was here tonight."

Pushed from the Trough
· TORONTO, 1834 ·

"Bloody bastards!"

Bill Mackenzie couldn't believe the message. After half a dozen years of fair and accurate reporting for His Majesty's Assembly, he was being canned. He read the letter again.

William Lyon Mackenzie
Editor
Daily Parish Pump
York

It has come to my attention on a number of occasions that you have been the author of articles in your newspaper which have been, shall I put it delicately, not altogether in the interests of my government. I have attempted to tolerate these articles as a vehicle of legitimate protest and as an outlet for imaginary grievances against my government.

However, your most recent scurillous and totally unfounded attacks upon me and my loyal councillors cannot be overlooked. I know nothing of the young lady to whom you referred, nor about the riot at the Allbalmy Club. As you know, the Liquor Control Board of Upper Canada has no control over bottomless dancing by the attorney-general.

Therefore, I have advised the clerk of the assembly that your employment as official Hansard reporter is officially terminated as of this day, and that henceforth you are to receive no further payments from this government.

I expect that in due course you will come to see the error of your ways and will realize that the system of government which you attack without cause is best for the continued growth and prosperity of the King's colonial province.

Yours truly,
Sir Pelegrine Maitland
Governor
Province of Upper Canada

Bill crumpled the letter in disgust. His first impulse was to rush to his quill pen to prepare fresh vitriol for next week's paper, but he kept his emotions in check. Instead, he decided to wander down to Montgomery's Tavern to see if his friend Colin was emptying another cask. He was.

"I know why you're here," Colin said. "I was fired too."

"Amazing, isn't it?" said Bill. "They deny there's a family compact, and then they do this. Bad enough I can't find an advertiser anywhere; now I've lost my reliable income as well. Bloody bastards. What do you suppose finally ticked them off?"

Colin shrugged. "Couldn't have been your attacks on antiquated liquor laws. You've been doing that for years. It was probably your piece on the appointment of Claude Backside to the Provincial Patronage Commission. That was pretty gross. 'An old fart brings gas to patronage commission.' He's not so old, you know."

"They deserved it. Imagine having the nerve to call it the Provincial Patronage Commission. They must think we're a bunch of dolts. They could at least call it the Governor's Liquor Licence Board, or the King's Municipal Board." Bill sipped his beer thoughtfully. "Y'know, Maitland went rangy when I did that number about his government buying a 25 per cent share of the lumber company, so's he could have a window on the lumber industry. It wasn't my fault the bottom fell out of the lumber market."

Colin sighed. "I don't know why they fired me."

Bill snorted. "You said Maitland should have gone into the feed business. You said he'd have made a fortune selling all that slop his filthy pig-faced morons slurp from the public trough. 'Patronage Pigs in a Putrid Pen.' I loved it."

Colin grinned. "Rather colorful, I thought, and accurate to boot. You think that offended him?"

"Well, let's say that he viewed it as somewhat less than totally objective."

"Watch it, Bill, you're starting to talk like him."

"Maybe it's all for the best then. If you hang around that assembly too long you start to believe that garbage. I've got to go write an editorial. It's going to be an objective, unbiased, and totally unemotional analysis of the unjust dismissal of a loyal public servant."

Colin smirked. "I expect the headline will be bland and inoffensive."

"Sure," said Bill. "'Falling off the Hind Tit' says it all."

NO._____

APPLICATION FORM
FAMILY COMPACT

Name: _____.
 (English Christian Name)   (Surname)

Current Address: _____.
 (state whether condominium, townhouse or Rosedale mansion)

Check other applicable properties: ( ) Florida condominium
 ( ) Muskoka Cottage
 ( ) International time share weeks
 ( ) Rental properties

Place of Birth: ( ) United Kingdom
 ( ) Other

Religion: ( ) Church of England
 ( ) Heathen

Education: ( ) Oxford
 ( ) Cambridge
 ( ) Colonial Illiteracy College

Heritage: LIST three titled ancestors within three generations. If not possible name two advertising executives in your immediate family.

Influential relatives: LIST six close relations of social standing in Town of York. In each case state whether Judge, Bishop, Minister of Crown, Owner of football team, owner of television station, owner of brewery.

(1)

Banks: LIST *two trust companies which you own.*

Trust Companies: LIST *which banks your trust companies own.*

Your Present Status: ( ) Fund raiser for Family Compact
( ) Chairman of public electrical utility
( ) Senator
( ) Ad agency owner
( ) Land developer
( ) Publisher

HAVE you ever had any personal relationship with William Lyon MacKenzie of the Town of York?

I hereby enclose a cheque for ( )$1,000, ( )$2,000, ( )$5,000, ( )$10,000, made out to Family Compact as my initiation fee, with the full understanding that said fee entitles me to nothing more than dinner at Winston's Restaurant in the Town of York should I be successfull in my application.

(signed) _____.

(Applicant.)

welcome to the family

A Golden Moment
of History

Every day for thirty years, Abner and the boys had gathered at Monty Montgomery's Tavern for a few beers and a little bragging. No rules, no regulations, no women. Nothing to interfere with a man's honest drinking.

But, ever the dutiful husbands, Abner and the boys would cut out after a few beers and head for the wives. Sometimes even their own.

Then the Liquor Licence Board of Upper Canada was formed and the lives of Abner and the boys changed forever.

"New rules, boys," said Monty, as he brushed aside a hanging plant to post a decree from the LLBUC beside the dart board. "You can't quaff[1] your favorite brew unless you qualify."

Abner snorted. "Monty, I've quaffed enough beer in this pigsty of yours to drown Toronto. Sometimes, when I step outside after a long night of drinking, I almost do. What do you mean, 'qualify'?"

"Sorry, LLBUC rules. It has to do with truth-in-advertising. Now that the breweries are aiming their beers at different markets, the Government wants to make sure that properly qualified peole are drinking the right beer. Otherwise, there's no truth in advertising."

"Sounds like a lot of bureaucratic crap to me," grumbled Abner. "Gimme a Blue."

"Okay, but you've got to show me your pilot's licence for your balloon."

"I don't have a balloon."

"There are other ways to qualify. Let's see . . . the LLBUC says Blue is available to people who play offbeat games, usually a combination of existing sports, such as grass skiing. Okay, here's a qualifying question: Explain the offside penalty in ice pinochle."

"How would I know? I've never played ice pinochle!"

"Tough. No Blue for you."

Abner scowled and slammed his fist on the bar. Monty turned to a newcomer. "What'll it be, Benjamin?"

"50."

"Sorry, Benjamin. No sunglasses."

"What?"

"You gotta have sunglasses. And let me see the ownership for your pickup truck."

"What ARE you talking about?"

"New LLBUC rules. Right over there on the wall. '50' drinkers gotta wear sunglasses and drive a man's pickup, to give some veracity[2] to Labubble Brewery's advertising."

"Monty, I don't usually bust up this tavern except on weekends, but I'm going to start early unless you serve me a 50, now. Or do me and the boys and our .45 have to convince you?"

"Sorry, rules are rules. I could lose my licence and then you'd have nothing to bust up but your wife's face. You don't like it, you go talk to the LLBUC."

"Might be a damn good idea." Benjamin surled over to the corner and huddled with Abner. After a minute, the two men slouched out the door in a snarl.[3]

Another regular stumbled to the bar as if to order, once his mind focussed. "Please, good sir, an Old Vienna."

Monty hesitated. "What's your game, Chester?"

"I don't play any games, sir. I merely pass my time by drinking."

"According to the LLBUC, people who drink O.V. know they've found their game, right from the first time they played. What's yours?"

"To humor you, sir, I'll say it's curling. Now would you please serve me an O.V.?"

"I'm obliged to ask you a qualifying question. Which national curling team won the silver broom in the 1798 Rawalpindi Brier?"

"Egypt."

"Wrong. Nepal. Try again tomorrow."

"Sir, I shall be obliged to find my game in law, pursuing my legal right to a drink to the limit, if necessary."

Dexter sauntered up to the bar, full of good humor and the previous tavern's fine brews.

"Dexie, old fellow, it's good to see you. How'd you find the place?"

"Ish easy. I followed the fire trucksh."

"Pardon me?"

"I followed the fire trucksh, like in the advertising. You're sold on Golden, you follow the fire trucksh to the barbecue. Where'sh the pool?"

"We're not having any barbecue and we don't have a pool."

"Musht have a pool. You got a pool ROOM."

"Dexter, do you want a Golden?"

"Yep, but I wanna warn you. You're breaking the law, you know. You can't serve Golden here. LLBUC regulation 324-C (viii) Subsection 84 Paragraph 16 Clause 72 (xlviii). I use those numbersh when I'm on the road, that'sh why they're called roamin' numerals. Anyway, you can't tell a dumb joke, you haven't got a pool, you haven't got a barbecue, and there ishn't a pretty girl anywhere in sight, near'sh I can shee, and I can't shee very far, shee? But there are no shes to shee."

Monty was dumbfounded. He checked the decree from the LLBUC, Regulation 324-C (viii) Subsecton 84 Paragraph 16 Clause 72 (xlviii): "No Golden shall be served where the owner of a tavern does not provide a barbecue lunch, a swimming pool, and a dozen pretty girls who neither drink nor sweat, but merely serve those who stand and wait."

"You stand and wait right here, Dexter. I've got to find some other guys to take care of this problem."

Monty tore out the door, and within moments Dexter heard muffled shouts from outside Montgomery's Tavern. "Atten-HUT! Aww-right, men, we're going to march down Yonge Street and run the LLBUC into Lake Ontario. By the right, quick, MARCH!"

As the hastily ordered Loyal Force of Monty's Revenge straggled off into the distance, Dexter weaved back and forth at the bar and pondered his role in history. The rebellion of 1837, fought over a barbecue and pretty maids all in a glow.

It was indeed a Golden moment.

[1]Quaff: Favorite jargon of headline writers. Four quaffs in a gaffon.
[2]Veracity: Typo of Vera City, the home of Labubble Brewery. Somewhere near Stratford.
[3]Snarl: A 19th-century device to assist unruly men to the door of a tavern. *See* Bouncer.

The Colonel and the Tart

Colonel John By expected to return home to London to a hero's welcome for his splendid achievement in constructing the Rideau Canal.

But before he could pack his skates and bid farewell forever to the Dow's Lake Winter Carnival in Bytown, a motley collection of snobbish gentlemen arrived in town. This collection was more formally known as the British Parliament's Colonial Boondoggling Committee, and it had travelled all the way to this remote colony to demand that Col. By explain his lengthy and vague expense account.

The inquisition was held in the basement of the Bytown National Tavern and Arts Centre.

"What's this item for travel to New York, Miami, and Venice all about?" asked Carlisle Thistle-Downey, MP for Worcestershire-Chutney.

"I had to look around at other canals, now didn't I? I'd never dug anything bigger than a drainage ditch on me father's farm, and you expect me to go off into the wilderness and build a trench deep enough for your royal bleedin' barges."

Thistle-Downey bristled. "I hear your locks aren't even built to British standards."

By stood his ground. "Bloody right they're not. We're not building bleedin' drainage ditches on the Suffolk plain, mate. We're doing it right."

Argyle Soxcotton, MP for Loverswhiff-Scandal, sniffed, "Eighteen pounds for 'Off'. What is 'Off'?"

"Mosquito repellent," said By. "If we could have harvested mosquitoes, we could have exported them by the ton to France. Good food for the froggies."

The committee members chuckled, but Soxcotton persisted. "You mean, your men couldn't stand a little mosquito bite?"

By was not intimidated. "No, sir, not Canadian mosquitoes. These bleedin' buggers were big and smart. They'd never fly if they could unzip the tent flap and walk right in. One night we lost our best cook when a swarm of them pulled out his tent pegs and carried away the mess tent, cook, stove and all."

Soxcotton was appalled. "Really?"

By pressed on. "Really. We tried throwing dynamite, but twern't no use. The buggers would catch it in their feet and drop it back on us. They'd come at us, swarm after swarm, picking off anyone careless enough to stray away from his 'Off.' If you look at the sentry roster, you'll see that we never posted sentries at night. We figured even the Yanks wouldn't be stupid enough to be out in the dark."

"Dear me, you underestimate American stupidity," Soxcotton muttered. By shrugged.

Houndstooth Shag, an MP from Barberry-Jam, harrumphed. "One thousand seven-hundred and fifty pounds for R and R. Explain, please."

By grinned. "Me and the boys were feeling a little randy one weekend, what with bein' back in the bleedin' bush for six months, so we chartered an ox-van and spent a few days in Montreal. It was good for morale."

Shag glowered. "Fifty pounds for 'companionship.' Explain, please."

By shuffled his feet. "It's just like it says, sir. Companionship in Montreal don't come cheap."

Shag murmured, "I see, I see. All I can say is that I expect an officer of the British army to be more inventive in the way he presents these items. In my day, we'd have called it therapeutic massage, or some such thing. I don't know what the world is coming to. Companionship, indeed. Sounds like the sort of thing the lower classes pick out of the newspaper."

By blushed. "Actually, sir, we did get a hint of it in a copy of the Montreal *Gazette* that came our way. I guess we shouldn't have been encouraged because, truth to tell sir, she wasn't exactly as advertised."

Shag, his eyes now bulging, demanded, "Explain."

"Well, sir, she called herself Monique de la Champagne. But when we looked her up, she was plain old Maisie Templeton, straight off the boat from London. Not your tasty French tart at all, sir, but a plain and simple cold English lass, which is not even a reasonable facsimile. Beg your pardon, sir."

But By knew he was in trouble. The committee immediately voted to rent an ox-van and set out for Montreal to explore the colonel's allegations of the merits of the French over the English. After a thorough probing, the committee was bound to condemn him for being disloyal to the Queen.

But at least he'd never have to dig another ditch.

Canada Cotton

· GEORGIA, 1864 ·

O.B. Jo, on the run for seven weeks as a self-emancipated refugee of involuntary, compulsory, and uncompensated employment, staggered into the Memphis terminus of the Underground Railway. It was 4 a.m. on June 4, 1864, a steamy and muggy summer's night. Dawn was flushing the eastern sky even as the night porter pulled the chain in the men's washroom.

O.B., his night camouflage rapidly losing its effectiveness in the rosy glow of first light, crept up to the ticket window. "Ah'd like a through ticket to Canada," he whispered to the clerk.

The clerk rolled his eyes, then yawned. "Uh-huh. Ever'body's goan Canada. What's so good about Canada? You work for nuthin' down here, but you're warm. You go to Canada, you work your butt off, the government takes ever'thin' and you're cold. How y'all wanna git there?"

O.B. whispered, "You know, underground railroad."

The clerk whistled. "Yeah, yeah, how else? We don't have no airplanes. There hasn't been a man born yet could invent a airplane. Of course, you goan on the underground. I mean, we got a lot of ways of travellin' on the underground. Like, this week we got a seat sale."

O.B. said, "I doan wanna buy no seat. I just wanna get to Canada."

Patiently, the clerk explained. "Okay, we got a deal. Reglar fare on the underground is $40; we got a sale where your seat cost you $20. Course, you gotta wait until next month, and you gotta stay two weeks before you come back."

O.B. glanced around the terminal. "I gotta go NOW, tonight, and I ain't never comin' back."

"Yeah, they all say that until winter. Okay, how 'bout excursion fare?"

"Hey, man, this ain't no excursion. Ah'm runnin' for my life."

"Oh, you're in a hurry! Why didn't you say so? Okay, we can dispense with the charter tours and the package deals. You goan school?"

"Uh, no, I ain't never been to no real school."

"Where'd you learn to talk like that?"

"Stephen Foster Linguistics Institute."

"Right. Been there myself. You ain't no student. No student fare. Man, you look wrinkled. How old are you?"

"Massa say I was born eighteen hundred and twenty-four."

"That'd make you forty. Too young for senior citizens rate. If you wanna save money, I can let you go stand-by."

"I been standin' by the massa for forty years. I ain't gonna stand by no longer. You get me on the next train to Canada."

"How about executive class? You get free drinks."

"What kind?"

"Mint julep. Doubles."

"No, no, no. Just get me on the train to Canada."

"You want to stop over?"

"No."

"Got a good deal for two nights in Buffalo."

"No."

"Hotel, all meals, weekend rental pony, $99."

"NO! One ticket, non-stop, Canada. Now."

"All right, all right. How bout first class?"

"Sure, sure, I'll pay you back when I pick the cotton next year. You think I got rich being a slave?"

"No, and the only white stuff you're gonna be movin' in Canada is snow."

PART II

The Age of the White Pine

The white pine, Ontario's arboreal symbol, represents the careful husbanding of our precious resources by our forefathers. That's why there are so few white pines. Traditionally, history books represent the period in Ontario's development between Confederation and the turn of the century as blank pages, from page 157 to page 193 (no illustrations). In the Age of the White Pine, Ontario began to mature. It learned how to make a fast buck by selling our resources to foreigners, and how to duck responsibility by blaming the new federal government.

The Queen's Pub Crawl

"Your Majesty, I beg leave to bother you with a trifling matter." It was the Colonial Secretary. He was always butting in when the Queen was having a good time at the Duke of York.

The Duke of York was not a societal friend, but a pub, featuring the finest bangers in all of London, to be washed down with pitchers of shandy.

"For goodness sake, what is it, Alfred?" demanded the Queen. He was such a bore. Yesterday it had been the matter of a thousand wogs bushwacking a regiment in South Africa. The regiment had escaped with frayed cuffs, after giving the wogs a permanent waive to their kinky customs. The day before that it was something about cows attacking sacred railroads in India.

"It's the Canadians," said the Colonial Secretary.

"Oh." Only the Queen could turn up her nose, without actually turning up her nose, when she pronounced a disapproving "oh." She pronounced it with four syllables, as "ay-ah-oh-oo." (Try it. "Ay-ah-oh-oo.")

In the context of discussing Canadians, her disapproval was as obvious as the nose on her face, or as audible as the "ohs" on her lips.

"Oh." She yawned in spite of her good breeding. "Just a minute. Albert, get me another shandy, will you? That's a good boy. Now, what do they want?"

"They want a capital, Your Majesty."

"Oh, bother. Thank you, Albert. Care for a game of darts?"

"No thank you, Your Majesty. I've brought the maps of Canada. If you'll just pick out a capital, I can put a packet on the next ship and they should be able to start building in a month."

The Colonial Secretary unrolled the map for the Queen. "I can't see it," she cried. "Pin it up on that wall. There, right over the dart board. Now, where would they like it?"

The Colonial Secretary sighed. "Well, Your Majesty, it's your choice."

"Didn't I give them Kingston already?"

"Yes, but it's too close to the Americans."

"What about Montreal?"

"It's too close to Paris, if you know what I mean."

"I don't suppose they'd take Cornwall."

"I don't think so."

"Rats. Oh, damn, Albert, give me those darts. Well, if they want me to pick a capital, I'll do it my way." The Queen closed her eyes and flung a red-white-and-blue dart at the map. "What'd I hit?"

"Er, Bytown, Your Majesty."

"Let me see. There's something wrong with your eyes, Mr. Secretary. That's not Bytown, that's Hull, across the river. Look, you can see a bit of blue ink between the dart and the dot for Bytown."

"Your Majesty, you never make mistakes, and it would have been a mistake to hit Hull."

"It would? Well, we wouldn't want the capital to go to Hull. Ha, ha, ha, ha! Get it? Let's just call that a practice throw. Okay, everybody back. Albert, get me another shandy. Here I go again. There. How'd I do?"

"Ogdensburg. I'm afraid that's an American town."

"Well, luv, that would never do, would it? Ah, ducky, let's you and I say I 'it Bytown and you take care of it from there."

"Thank you, Your Majesty. I'll be putting this message in the overseas packet tonight."

"Wait a minute. Bytown. Is that place named after that scalliwag John By? The bloke who wasted a fortune digging a ditch through some swamp?"

The Colonial Secretary chose his words carefully. "Yes, ma'am, Colonel John By, who supervised the construction of the Rideau Canal."

"Ree-doo Canal. Took him too long and he spent too much and the Yankees never did attack 'im. Well, we can't 'ave 'is name on it. Wot's Bytown anyway?"

"I believe it's a lumber camp, Your Majesty."

"Right, then. Whaddya think we oughta call it. Something Indian-sounding, we oughta, oughta we? Yeah, oughta we. I mean we oughta. Well, Mr. Secretary, you work on it."

"Yes, Your Majesty." He removed the map, bowed once to the Queen, and left the pub. Oughta-we. If it was good enough for Her Majesty, it was good enough for the Canadians. Oughta-we it would be. It could have been worse, though. It could have been Hull.

He whistled softly to himself. He loved determining the course of history. Someday the Canadians would thank him.

One's as Bad
as Another

A sharp knock at the cabin door snapped Jean-Pierre Reigenstrief out of his nap by the fireplace. He uncurled himself from his bottle, stretched, and stepped over Old Blue, his favorite hound named after his favorite beer. The dog was sprawled by the fire, engrossed in the latest edition of *The Police Gazette*.

Yawning, Reigenstrief padded across the cabin's dirt floor. He opened the door to find a tousle-haired young man carrying a lantern in one hand and a clipboard in the other.

"Good evening, sir," said the young fellow cheerfully. "I'm conducting a poll of public opinion on Canada's very first election. Do you mind if I come in? I'd like to ask you a few questions."

Regenstrief hesitated, then he motioned the young man inside. The pollster went right to work. "If an election were to be held tomorrow, would you support Macdonald?"

Reigenstrief raised his eyebrows. "Ain't gonna be no election tomorrow. It's next month. Everybody knows that."

"Yes, yes, but let's pretend," urged the pollster. "Suppose this were the day before the election. Would you be supporting Macdonald?"

"That all depends," said Reigenstrief slowly. "Which Macdonald you talking about?"

The pollster checked his notes. "John Macdonald."

Reigenstrief yawned again, and scratched his hip. "Is that the John Macdonald that drinks, or not?"

"I'm quite sure he drinks, but that's irrelevant, unless you're a teetotaler, then I guess it isn't." The pollster was becoming a little unhappy, with his hair becoming progressively more tousled.

"Well, all right, let's put it this way," Reigenstrief said. "How do you spell his name?"

The pollster checked his clipboard again. "J-O-H-N."

Old Blue rattled *The Police Gazette* noisily and rolled his eyes towards the ceiling. Reigenstrief patted the hound to assure him that everything was under control. "I meant the last name."

"Oh." The pollster turned quite red in the face. "M-A-C-D-O-N-A-L-D."

49

Reigenstrief winced. "That doesn't tell me much. Is that a big 'd' or a little 'd'?"

The pollster glanced at his clipboard. "Oh, yes," he smiled, relieved at getting an easy question, "that's a little 'd', unless you mean the one after the 'c'."

Old Blue growled and crumpled the paper into a ball. The pollster backed warily towards the door. "Don't mind him," Reigenstrief said. "He gets that way in the presence of nincompoops, but he's not dangerous, just impolite. Now, so far we have a poll for either John Macdonald or John Macdonald, is that right?"

The pollster ran three fingers through his tousled hair. The other two were worn down to stubs from a lifetime of checking off "no opinion." "Uh, yeah, I guess you're right. So which will it be?"

Reigenstrief asked, "Well, are we talking about Ontario or are we talking about Canada?"

The pollster turned to page 5 on his clipboard. "It says here, the election of the federal parliament and the legislature of the province of Ontario."

Old Blue growled again. Reigenstrief shushed him. "That could be either John Macdonald or John Macdonald. Have you got a middle name for him on that fancy polling sheet of yours?"

The pollster checked pages 7 through 15. On 16, he found a clue. "Yes, it's Alexander."

"Oh," Reigenstrief cried. "Now we're getting somewhere. That's the name of the guy running for prime minister. John Alexander Macdonald."

"Oh, oh," said the pollster. "There's a whole page of instructions here. 'Caution: Alexander is the middle of name of Macdonald referred to on pages 1, 3, 4, 7, 10, and 11. Sandfield is the middle name of the Macdonald in all other questions. Refer to questionnaire form 14-C, Subsection (a)'."

The pollster shuffled papers and found form 14-C. "'Under no circumstances is the pollee—that's you—to be given a hint by the poller—that's me—as to the identity of the Macdonald in any of the questions. Clarification only leads to informed opinions.'"

Old Blue growled louder. "Nice doggy," stammered the pollster. "Nice doggy. Macdonald, little d, John and John, Alexander and Sandfield, all love nice doggies."

Reigenstrief turned his back. The tousled-hair pollster's fate was doomed. Old Blue would do what fair-minded dogs always do to polls.

We Almost All
Love a Parade

"Let me get this straight," said the tall, bespectacled clerk in the Department of Public Parades and Miscellaneous Nuisances. "You want a licence to hold a 'walkingthon'?"

The thin young man on the other side of the counter fingered his beard nervously. "A walk-a-thon."

The clerk peered over the frames of his wire glasses. "Boy, this is Toronto, 1885. I may be getting old and maybe I haven't kept up with the times, but I have no idea what a walkingthon is."

The young man seized the opportunity to instruct one of his elders. "Well, it's like a parade. I raise money this way. For every mile I walk, you pay me a certain amount of money. If you promise a dollar a mile, and I walk 10 miles, you pay me $10."

The clerk sneered. "Not likely. That's a week's pay. I could walk the ten miles myself and save $10. I could walk 20 miles and save $20. Hell, I could keep on walking forever and never have to work again."

The young man smiled. "It doesn't work that way. The money isn't for me. I'm trying to build a fund for a good cause."

"Ah, a good cause, is it? Well, well, Toronto the Good is always in favor of charity. Now, assuming this cause of yours is legitimate—and mind you, we'll have an inspector check it out—when do you want to hold this walking throng?"

"Walk-a-thon. I'd like to organize it for July 12."

The clerk put down his quill. "July 12. That's a pretty busy day in Toronto. We've only got a limited parade-licence quota, and it's just about used up on July 12. The Queen herself would have trouble getting a licence. Why, we've got more Orangemen in Toronto that day than there are bingo games in Quebec. We could defeat all the Pope's forces and still have enough left over to invade Ireland. But don't get me wrong, lad. Those parades are really part of the peace movement. You know our slogan, 'Boyne the Bomb!'"

The young fellow shrugged. "Well, that's why I want my Walk-a-thon on July 12. There are going to be a lot of people in the city. People are usually generous on a holiday, and I think I can raise a lot more money when there are a lot of good-hearted Orangemen around. They are good-hearted, aren't they?"

The clerk smiled gently. "Of course we are. Of course we are. Tell you what, you seem like a good lad, even if you do have some peculiar ideas about raising money, so I'm going to recommend your parade licence."

Much relieved, the young man grinned. "Thank you very much."

"One more thing," the clerk said. "What's your good cause?"

The young man beamed. "The Louis Riel Defence Fund."

Dear Ollie

John A. Macdonald
Prime Minister of Canada
Ottawa

My dear John:
We seem to be on the verge of a constitutional crisis, which I believe is of your own making. You insisted on retaining control over the liquor industry which, I understand, is difficult enough in your private life. Well, my dear fellow, the churches and the women in Ontario are causing me more headaches than you have ever felt on a bottle of gin.

They want me to prohibit strong drink. Now, I know this is exactly what you feared. Since Ottawa lies in the province of Ontario—for that matter, it lies everywhere on practically anything—prohibition of alcoholic beverages would affect you profoundly. How could you face that Tory caucus of yours every day without the fortitude of the bottle?

Well, you need not worry for the moment. The women have no votes in Ontario, thank God, and the churchmen are only doing their duty from the pulpit. As long as there is a secret ballot, your bottle shall be safe.

Sincerely,
Oliver Mowat
Prime Minister of Ontario

* * *

Oliver Mowat
Prime Minister of Ontario
Toronto

Dear Oliver:
I know you did not write a letter about prohibition merely to tweak my conscience about my drinking. The fact that you assure me everything is all right in Ontario suggests that I should begin hoarding liquor immediately. What is the problem?

John A. Macdonald
Prime Minister of Canada

Dear John:

Since you have now poked your nose into Ontario's affairs, I shall tell you about the prohibition movement. The girls at Owen Sound have organized a Canadian branch of the Women's Christian Temperance Movement. Now, these ladies aren't too much bother for, as I said in my earlier letter, they don't vote.

It's the churchmen. The Methodists, the Presbyterians, and the Baptists would have us dumping all spirits into Lake Ontario tomorrow. Fortunately, the Catholics and Anglicans, who fill the chalice with fortified grape juice, are standing firm against "temperance."

As you know, I don't really care for alcoholic drink myself, since I am an abstainer. However, I do fear for my country's future if my prime minister were denied his wee drappy in the mornin'.

Neither you nor I can afford to let this movement grow. Therefore, I suggest I pass the buck to you. Well, dear John, it was you who wanted control of the liquor industry. We're just a bunch of county boys down here at the Ontario Legislature.

Sincerely
Oliver Mowat
Prime Minister of Ontario

* * *

Dear Ollie:

Come, come, no need to get nasty. Just keep stalling. I always say that a good rum makes a good man out of a bad one, and vice versa. Take the very best from your distilleries and spill the stuff into the tap water. Get your people happy! A happy voter cares not about the constitution.

Yours truly,
John
PM

Dear John:

I have decided to implement prohibition on an experimental basis. During the next year, no alcoholic beverages shall be permitted to be sold in the County of Carleton. As you are well aware, that is the county in which the capital is located.

I realize that the proximity of Quebec makes this limited prohibition impossible to police, but then the choice does become yours. Do you wish to be seen as a law-abiding citizen of Ontario, or do you wish to be seen as a Conservative prime minister (the twitching of Louis Riel's body still fresh in the public's mind), forced to feed his habit with alcoholic transfusions from Quebec?

> Sincerely
> Oliver Mowat
> Prime Minister of Ontario

* * *

Dear Ollie:

You play a mean game of politics. All right, you force my hand, which this morning is quaking and quivering but not with excitement. I shall take direct and concrete federal action in this matter. That is, I shall refer it to the courts for a decision as to whether you, I, or anyone else can prohibit the sale of alcoholic beverages. God, I hope not!

> Yours truly
> John A. Macdonald
> Prime Minister of Canada

* * *

Dear John:

To the courts? Chicken!

Sincerely
Ollie

Sons of the Soil

"Good afternoon, Hewers Ontario. May I help you?"

"Uh, I must have the wrong number. I don't want any girls, I want the Upper Canada Investment Agency."

"You have it, sir. We've changed our corporate name."

"Oh. Well, this is Red Cheval of Revere, Cheval and Ryder in Boston, Massachussets. We're interested in making a bundle . . . er, investing in the development of your province of Ontario. I was wondering if your agency could advise us on the juiciest, that is, the more suitable areas for investment."

"Certainly, sir. I'll put you through to Grant Giveaway, our foreign investment consultant."

"Hello, Giveaway here."

"Mr. Giveaway, my name is Red Cheval of Revere, Cheval and Ryder in Boston, Massa . . . "

". . . chusetts, and you want to make a fast buck on juicy land speculation in Upper Canada. You Yanks are all the same. You think we're a bunch of backwoods hillbillies up here, prepared to sell our heritage for a few lousy American dollars. Well, I want to tell you, we've got our pride. That's what this agency is all about. How much money you got to spend?"

"A hundred million."

"That'll buy a lot of pride. In fact, that'll buy all the pride in York County, Simcoe County, Grey County, and most of Middlesex. That's down London-way, you know. What are you interested in?"

"Our slogan is, 'One million if buy land, two million if buy apartments." We'll look at anything we can buy from Canadians to sell back to Canadians and make an honest Yankee dollar."

"Sounds fair to me. All I've got to do is make sure our government gets a cut along the way."

"Hey, look fella, we know all about governments. We've even got a special fund for governments. One per cent of every transaction is donated to the governing party. We fill out a very generous cheque."

"Don't tell me about it, write it."

"You want the cheque in advance?"

"No, no, that was just a figure of speech. I used to be a reporter on the

York *Daily Metro Sunstar.* Sometimes the old cliches pop out when I get excited."

"Oh. You had me worried that I was dealing with an honest government."

"Not a chance. Look, I've got a whole catalogue of stuff here. You want to buy some timber rights? Still lots of white pine around but it's going fast. Someday it'll be all gone and they'll turn it into the provincial tree or some damn thing."

"No, not timber."

"How about a nice iron ore deposit? We've got tons of them in eastern Ontario."

"No, no. Forestry and mining and stuff like that is too much work. The only thing we want to smudge our hands with is filthy lucre. We don't mind a few ink stains from signing deeds, but don't put us in a forest. Slivers are painful."

"A man after my own heart. Tell you what you do. You come in, look over the land around London, and buy what you like. We'll just keep a running tab and when it looks like public opinion is starting to boil, we'll tell you when to stop."

"What then?"

"Then? Oh, nothing. The lieutenant-governor will make some obligatory noises about foreigners buying up Canadian soil, but don't worry about it. He has his job to do."

"Thank you so much. Revere, Cheval and Ryder is indebted to you for your kind assistance."

"One more thing. There's a thousand acres on the banks of the Thames, just north of London, that I've had my eye on for some time. If you could ... "

"Consider it done. I like the way you Canadians do business. You're so much like us."

Buyers and Sellers

"Now then, Eaton," snapped Sellers, "let's get to the truth. What's your game?"

Eaton looked around Sellers' office, bewildered. He had been invited to the Department of Consumer Skewering and Price Fudging to discuss his new policy of guaranteeing satisfaction or refunding money. He thought his policy was a grand innovation, and he couldn't understand the frosty reception he was getting from the bureaucracy.

"I don't understand, Mr. Sellers," Eaton said. "I thought you wanted to discuss my new policy."

"Oh, I do, I do," growled Sellers. "But let's not pretend you're doing anybody any favors. What're you up to?"

Eaton was flummoxed. "I don't know what you mean. I thought that if I could guarantee satisfaction, I could attract more customers. Maybe I'll go broke if people take advantage of me, but I doubt it."

Sellers laughed. "C'mon, c'mon, don't give me that guff. We see new scams every day. Usually they're blatantly transparent and we clean them up in a hurry. But I don't mind telling you, you've got us stumped."

Eaton smiled. "Maybe it's just what it appears to be."

"It appears to be a fraud, that's what it appears to be," Sellers snarled. "I just haven't figured out how."

Eaton said, "Why don't you try the policy for yourself?"

"We have," Sellers spat. He pulled a thick file from his desk drawer, and began leafing through it. "We've been checking your place out pretty thoroughly, as a matter of fact. We've had people in every day, buying stuff, and then bringing it back. I'll give you a few examples."

"Filcher went in on a Monday, bought a garden hoe, then brought it back Tuesday morning complaining that the hoe handle was too long. How can a hoe handle be too long? You didn't tell him to grip it closer to the blade, you gave him his money back."

Sellers shuffled some more. "Grabsley went in on a Wednesday and bought a gallon of white paint. He brought back part of the gallon on Thursday, claiming the stuff dripped when he threw it at the ceiling. You gave him his money back."

Sellers pulled out another report. "Drimbobble bought a goldfish on

Friday, but came back on Saturday complaining that the fish died when he turned on the blender. And you gave him his money back."

Eaton chuckled. "Well, I wasn't going to sell him another fish. If he wants a blenderized tuna salad sandwich he can always come to my cafeteria."

"The point is, Eaton, that you're up to something. Your policy is creating havoc on lower Yonge Street. The other merchants have been on my ass, demanding that we do something to wipe this filthy policy from the streets of Toronto. Now, either you stop the policy, or we'll continue to harrass . . . er, monitor your operation with large scale purchases and returns. If you don't clean up your act we'll . . . we'll . . . we'll . . ."

Eaton smiled. "Take me over, like a trust company?"

"Yes, dammit, if we have to! Do you understand?"

Eaton shrugged. "I think so. By the way, when Filcher came back the second time, he bought a roto-tiller instead of another hoe. Grabsley bought a paint sprayer, two gallons of paint, a dozen rolls of wallpaper, plus a sofa and chair to match. And Drimbobble went home with a new gas barbecue grill when I convinced him that blenderized goldfish are dreadful. They always seem to take on the taste of carrot juice. Good-day, Mr. Sellers."

The Permafrost Pioneer

Guelph, Oct. 15, 1882

Dear Father:

I realize how much you wish one of your sons could be a man of the soil, but I fear you have chosen wrong in choosing me. I think my tuition fees to the Ontario Agricultural College here shall amount to an outright donation on your behalf. I never liked the taste of spinach, let alone had any desire to grow it. I know all about hops, at least in liquid form. As for the anatomy of a cow, it is the hind teat from which I seem to be sucking in the class standings.

Your son,
Theodore

Guelph, April 17, 1883

Dear Father:
I have completed one year of studies here at OAC. So far I have learned that eggs do not freeze well in the shell, and that one uses caution in approaching a milking cow. My love life has suffered severely as a result of my ignorance.

Your son,
Theodore

* * *

Guelph, May 3, 1884

Dear Father:
My worst fears have been realized. I have successfully completed the agriculture course here at Guelph. I realize from your last letter that I am not to come home to the bank. Since you expect me to become a farmer, Father, perhaps you could use your position as bank chairman to provide a loan to start me in the business of agriculture.

Your son,
Theodore

* * *

Guelph, May 10, 1884

Dear Father:
Thank you for your most speedy response to my request for a loan. No, I have no collateral. I'm a recent graduate. If I had any collateral I would sell it and avoid your bank. I am pleased to hear that if I ever become a successful farmer, the bank would be delighted to do business with me.

Your son,
Theodore

New Liskeard, March 21, 1912

Dear Father:
Since I was unable to secure a bank loan from you or any of your colleagues, I was forced to take a laborer's job for twenty-eight years to save up for a farm. I hope I have not forgotten how to split peas and shell wood. As you can see, I have not bought a farm in southern Ontario where speculators and other bankers have driven the price of farmland out of reach.

Through the Ontario government, I have received a substantial grant to develop a farm on the Clay Belt around here. I have my doubts about its worth, for as far as I can determine, there are no lands hereabouts yet owned by the banks.

Your son,
Theodore

* * *

New Liskeard, Sept. 19, 1912

Dear Father:
I am weary to the bone as I write this letter. Since sun-up this morning I have been shovelling snow. This will be my longest winter, by far.

Your son,
Theodore

* * *

New Liskeard, June 20, 1913

Dear Father:
Yesterday I bought tomato plants. Today I broke a shovel trying to dig the frozen ground. Life is harsh in the north but Premier Whitney, bless his bottomless treasury, assures me this land is arable. Last week I received another government cheque to tide me over the summer. It was drawn on your bank.

Your son,
Theodore

New Liskeard, July 22, 1913

Dear Father:
I finally got those tomato plants into the ground. Amelia and I kept them alive in the south window until the ground thawed on Monday. I think the farm is turning out all right.

> Your son,
> Theodore

* * *

New Liskeard, Aug. 4, 1913

Dear Father:
Amelia almost cried as she picked frozen green tomatos this morning. There must be a recipe for pre-cast tomato relish. Ask mother, if she has one, to send it along. Another cheque from Whitney came in the mail. The post office is the only cash crop I have.

> Your son,
> Theodore

* * *

New Liskeard, May 7, 1914

Dear Father:
You will be delighted to learn that I have finally discovered a future in farming. Amelia and I have decided to turn over the farm to your bank and return to the south. I have accepted a research position at the Ontario Agricultural College where I shall devote the rest of my life to developing tomato plants that can grow to maturity in two weeks. I figure that if the Government wants to pay me to grow tomatos, I might as well do it where it's warmer. Thank you for all your help.

> Your son,
> Theodore

PART III

The Age of the Blue Jay

Ontario's avian emblem is a raucous, noisy creature, a fitting representative of the first half of the 20th century. This could also be called the Age of Pestilence, for in this period Ontario was visited by many plagues: The First World War, The Second World War, the Great Depression, and Premier Mitch Hepburn.

The Grand Trunk
Slammed Shut

On a hot and sultry August day in rural Leeds, the Forfar stationmaster checked his watch again. The noon train was late. Not that the noon train ever came at noon. It usually got in around 13:15, but it was already 14:30 and there was not a smudge of smoke on the faded blue horizon.

It had been that way ever since the government set up Via Grand Trunk.

The stationmaster shrugged. It didn't really matter. The only passenger in the station was Mrs. Hettie McJacques who had bought a through-ticket to the end of the line at Westport, about twenty miles along. But all Mrs. McJacques had waiting for her in Westport was a drunken husband who would thrash her for being late. Next time in, she'd threaten to sue the railway for personal damages.

She'd gone to court once, where Judge Orval O'Neally threw out the case on the grounds that the train was always late. He said that if it ever came in on time, a lot of people would sue for breach of promise because they would have gone to the station at the usual time, only to find that the train had let them down by being on time and leaving early.

The stationmaster sighed. The Brockville, Westport, and Sault Ste. Marie had held a lot of promise. It had been built during the heyday of the iron rail, when railroads criss-crossed the United States and railways plunged headfirst into the Canadian swamp, often to sink out of sight in a morass of bank debts.

The BW and SSM ran into a similar problem. The obstacle wasn't a swamp. It was a hill. The railway started at B, got as far as W, but never approached SSM. At W, it encountered a mound of rock known as Westport Mountain. And it became the little railway that couldn't.

The telegraph clicked, then spat out a torrent of clicks and clacks that the stationmaster hastily jotted down on a pad of paper.

"Mrs. McJacques? I got bad news for you. The train ain't comin'."

"What's that? Listen, if I don't ever get home, my husband's going to kill me when I do. Where is it?"

"It's in Lyndhurst. It ain't ever comin' here again, and it ain't going back to Brockville. It's stuck. The government has closed the line."

At the sound of "government," Mrs. McJaques spat on the station floor. "Damn Liberals. Why, that pack of fools wouldn't know a train from an oxcart. How do they expect me to get home?"

"I dunno, Mrs. McJaques. Maybe they'll send a bus. I must say, this is pretty mean of them, what with all the help you've given them over the years."

He chuckled. Mrs. McJaques was a fifth-generation Tory. There wasn't a Liberal within fifty miles of Westport. The last one through Forfar was a big cheese who had been arrested for misappropriating railway tickets. He'd been wearing police bracelets at the time.

"I guess it had to come, Mrs. McJaques. This decision, I mean, not the train. It ain't never comin. See, 'cept for you, nobody rides this train anymore. You can't expect the Liberals to keep shovelling money into a railway that only runs in a Tory riding, can you?"

Mrs. McJaques snuffled. "Herm's gonna kill me, I tell you. Maybe this time I can get some money outta the railway. The judge said I could expect it to be on time by being late, but he didn't say it had a right to be so late it never ran again."

The Evolution of the Automobile in Ontario

by MANIFOLD KRANKSCHAFT

October, 1902. First automobile sold in Ontario. Immediately put up on blocks for the winter.

April 2, 1903. First automobile taken for spin around the block.

April 2, 1903. Second automobile sold in Ontario. Proud owner meets owner of first automobile. Damage $300.

April 3, 1903. Automobile insurance offered for first time.

April 4, 1903. Automobile insurance rates hiked because of high accident rates (100 per cent of insured vehicles).

April 5, 1903. Government announces system of licences to control proliferation of automobiles.

April 6, 1903. Government introduces road tax on gasoline.

May 17, 1903. Owners of all vehicles in Ontario, both of them, form the Ontario Automobile Association, a lobby group, to demand better road maps.

May 18, 1903. Government says it can't afford to produce road maps. Hikes gasoline tax.

May 24, 1903. Both automobile owners take to the road for long weekend. Traffic jam in Muskoka as both try to occupy same road north of Orillia. OAA pressures government for superhighway.

June 1, 1903. Government says it can't afford superhighways. Raises gasoline tax.

September 23, 1903. First road paved in Ontario.

September 24, 1903. Pothole develops in new pavement. Owner No. 1 breaks spring. Sues government. Government settles. Raises gasoline tax.

September 25, 1903. First pothole repaired in Ontario.

September 26, 1903. Government launches investigation into cheap highway contract.

March 21, 1904. Government gets idea to build superhighway between Toronto and Hamilton. Has no cars to fill it, so puts Ford plant in Oakville and McLaughlin plant in Oshawa.

March 22, 1904. Assembly line spews cars out of Oakville. Trees not yet cleared from superhighway right-of-way. Damage, $4,321.34

March 23, 1904. First auto body shop opens in Ontario. Insurance rates hiked.

May 1, 1904. Owner of first automobile decides to get another. First used car salesman begins career in Ontario.

May 2, 1904. Used car salesman's brother hops into car and heads west to make huge profit on broken down heap in Calgary. Succeeds.

May 3, 1904. Owner of first automobile buys another. Complains about rising prices.

May 4, 1904. First new car recall in Ontario. Wheels fall off over 15 mph.

May 16, 1904. First woman drives car in Ontario.

May 17, 1904. First crude joke about women drivers appears in morning newspaper.

May 18, 1904. First letter to editor protesting newspaper's jokes about women is printed.

May 19, 1904. First woman driver meets proud owner of new car. Damage $550.26. Insurance rates rise.

June 29, 1904. First owner and first woman driver marry. First two-car family in Ontario. Don Mills not far away.

November 12, 1904. Owner of second car skids off road into tree after ice storm. First road salt company formed.

November 13, 1904. First automobile undercoating shop opens.

November 20, 1904. Owner of second car complains about high cost of simple repairs. Opens first Canadian Tire store. Offers first $9.95 tune-up special.

July 18, 1932. First radio commercial for auto dealer. Hot day. Does commercial in shorts.

July 19, 1952. First television commercial for auto dealer. Hot day. Does commercial in shorts, polka-dot shirt, red bow tie, candy-stripe jacket, straw hat, and black rubber boots, carries a white duck under one arm and a brown pig under the other, smokes a Cuban cigar and says, "Trust me".

Painting Pines

In a cold and dismal basement studio on Toronto's McCaul Street, a class of aspiring artists shivered through a critical analysis of their latest works. They were at the mercy of Antonio Bengo, a second-rate Italian artist who was working off his passage to Canada with a year's instruction at the Ontario Cottage of Art.

"Wottsa matter you guys!" Antonio moaned. "You no usa the brush lika European artists. You gotta lotsa nice girls in Toronto to paint, but you guys, you gotta go off to the bush up north to paint pine trees."

He strode quickly across the studio, and snatched up a few canvases leaning against the wall. "Looka this. Who didda this? Johnston. Hey, Johnston, what makesa you think people wanta look at pine trees?"

Johnston shrugged. "I like looking at pine trees. They strike a mood with me. It's a wilderness, an emptiness of the North, that I try to convey."

"Bah! Here'sa one from Jackson. More pine trees. Jackson, you can't even draw a pine tree. You gotta alla branches coming offa the one side."

Jackson groaned. "That's the way they grow."

"I donta care how they grow. It'sa notta what people wanta see. It no looka like a tree."

Bengo picked up another swatch of effort. "Lismer. Ah, yeah, Lismer. Paints like he's afraid of the canvas. Looka this. Each leaf a daub of paint. Dip, dip, dip. You gonna paint trees, you paint them like they were real. This looks lika you were squishing fleas with your brush."

Suddenly, Bengo ran across the room and tore a painting off the wall. "Harris, what'sa this? Looks like a mound of sherbet, melting under a 10-watta bulb. No detail. Tella me, what's its name?"

Harris squirmed in his seat. "Pic Island."

"Peeg Island. It'sa pile of pork?"

"No, no. Pic. P-I-C."

"I was right. Itsa pig. Or maybe, itsa dog."

Harris scowled. "I think it's quite all right."

"Oh, maybe so, if you wanta sell to Eskimos. Tell me, boys, why don't you ever go outa west to paint?"

Harris, Varley, Jackson, Harris, Macdonald, Johnston, and Lismer all snickered. This Bengo was a looney.

Varley spoke up. "What am I going to paint on the Prairies? I draw a line across the centre of the canvas, and I paint the top half blue and the bottom half green. If it were paint-by-number, I'd only have to count to two. I could even paint the top half of the canvases blue before I went, to cut down on my time."

Jackson, Harris, Macdonald, and Johnston bobbed their heads in agreement. "Right, there's nothing out there. Buffalo chips. Prairie grass. Maybe paint the wheat gold in autumn."

Bengo held up his hand for silence. "Whatta you think of this painter Emily Carr? She paints in the west."

A loud groan echoed around the room. "Ah, she's just a woman."

Bengo challenged them. "She paintsa trees, like you guys."

Jackson bristled. "Yes, but she paints straight trees. That's easy. You just run your brush up and down the canvas a few times, and you got a tree. Me, I've got to dab away like crazy and get all those branches on the same side of the pine. Sometimes I lie down when I'm painting to get the best perspective. That's the difference between Georgian Bay and Vancouver Island. Bent trees. I'll bet Carr couldn't paint a bent pine to save her life."

Bengo frowned. "Alla same, I donta think you guys is so great. You live in a new country, you builda a new civilization, you create a new culture. And alla you wanta do isa go into the bush and painta trees. I think I go backa to Italy and painta the girls."

The World at Your Beck and Call

When Adam Beck stuck two wires into the wall of his workshop, he discovered Ontario Hydro! Then he put a handle on the wires and invented the BECK POWER PLUG.

Unfortunately, he had a little trouble convincing people that he had invented anything worthwhile, so he helped Hydro set up its first mass advertising campaign:

AMAZING NEW POWER DEVICE
The INVENTION of the CENTURY!!
The Beck Power Plug will end your chores forever!

Unbelievable but true! The BECK POWER PLUG has been rated "Invention of the Century" by the renowned Association of Toasters, Waffle Irons, and Blender Lobbyists of America (Canada) Inc.

This in itself is *unbelievable*! What makes it absolutely *Incredible* is that it was invented in *Canada*, and there are no Japanese copies available yet.

The BECK POWER PLUG will change your life. As soon as you attach the BECK POWER PLUG to any machine, you begin to lead a life formerly the private preserve of the idle rich.

Here's what inventor **Adam Beck** says about his Power Plug:

"I only want all of mankind to share in what I have wrought. I could have made a million dollars by exploiting this amazing device, but I opted to improve the lot of all mankind by offering this simple little item to everyone."

And here is what happy users of the BECK POWER PLUG have to say:

George Enright, *farmer, Teeswater, Ont.*: "My family has been doing nothing but milking cows for generations. But Elsie, the wife, and I have become the euchre champions of Huron County since we installed the BECK POWER PLUG. We've taken our hands from under the cows and laid them back on the card table. And our cows have never been more content. It tickles their udders just to think of being milked electrically."

Mildred Carstairs, *housewife, Elmira, Ont.*: "I used to hate hauling ice blocks for the cook stove and raking ashes out of the ice box. Or was it the other way around? No matter, because since I bought the BECK POWER PLUG I've had time to improve my quilting and take three red ribbons at the Elmira Fall Fair. I used to be the laughing stock of the quilting section, but not any more, thanks to the BECK POWER PLUG."

Alfred Shiny Canoe, *Atikokan, Ont.*: "My life was one long nightmare of escorting American fishermen around pristine northern lakes and hauling in heavy, slippery, smelly fish to make money. But the BECK POWER PLUG changed all that when the acid rain killed the fish. Now all I have to do to make money is cash the Government cheque."

Maurice de Torrie, *chef, Toronto*: "At the Albany Club, where I prepare meals for the most influential stomachs in the province, the BECK POWER PLUG has been a boondoggle—I mean, a boon. It has figured in some way in almost every decision made over lunch at the Club. Many a mind has been changed and many a stomach turned by the use of the BECK POWER PLUG."

Thurmond Nukehead, *chairman, Atomic Explosions of Canada Limited, Ottawa*: "In the first ten years of operation, no nuclear BECK POWER PLUG has melted down."

Thousands of other testimonials are on file for examination at the head office of the Beck Power Plug Corporation. Unfortunately, for security reasons we are not able to tell you the address of the Corporation, but it is in a SAFE PLACE! Have we ever lied to you?

Bonus Testimonial! The BECK POWER PLUG is *Guaranteed* by the *Government of Ontario*!! You cannot ask for a truer blue-ribbon promise of quality.

Adam Beck knows the value of this promise: "I have been dealing with the Ontario Government for many years. They have never questioned my motives, nor have they attempted to interfere in my affairs. In fact, the Premier himself has assigned his best friends to help me. Their loyalty has helped make the BECK POWER PLUG what it is today."

The BECK POWER PLUG! Absolutely *Incredible*! Currently, the world's most startling discovery!

The BECK POWER PLUG! Send no money down, just pay for life!

A Niagara of contentment awaits you when you purchase the BECK POWER PLUG!

The Down and Out Mitch Heartburn

NOVEMBER, 1943.
Office of the New Drew Employment Agency

"Name, please."

"Hepburn. Mitchell Frederick Hepburn. Call me Mitch."

"Occupation?"

"Politician."

"That's not much."

"Mitch."

"It's not much, Mitch. Be more specific."

"Premier."

"First-class? Don't over-rate yourself."

"No, I was a premier."

"Oh. Province?"

"Ontario."

"Reason for unemployment?"

"I quit my job."

"Oh-oh. Mr. Hellburn, we have a hard time finding new work for people who quit."

"Hepburn. I had good reasons. There was a Liberal government."

"Whose?"

"Mine."

"You didn't get along with your own government?"

"Nope. And I'm proud to say I didn't get along with the other one, either."

"Which one?"

"The one in Ottawa. King's."

"The King is in England."

"Not that King. The nut that lives in Ottawa."

"My word, Mr. Hepburn, you will be a tough one to employ. You don't seem to get along well with your superiors or your government."

"I can do other things. I was an auctioneer once."

"Oh, really. Cattle, furniture, or land?"

"Government limousines."

"I thought you were the premier."

"I was. That's why I sold the limousines. It was the Depression."

"I'll bet it was, especially for your ministers on their bicycles. We don't have much call for limousine auctioneers."

"I can make speeches, sell stuff, that sort of thing. I gave one of my best speeches from a manure spreader."

"Did it die?"

"Did what die?"

"The shit when you shot it."

"Don't get smart. This is wartime. Do you want a good propagandist?"

"You do like fighting a lot. What did you fight with King about?"

"The war. I didn't like the way he was running it."

"How would you run it?"

"Faster."

"Machine guns on the limousines, no doubt. Mr. Heifer, have you ever done any social work?"

"Hepburn. My boy, I was a politician. Half a politician's life is social work. Why I was a fount of social reform, an activist for the working man. Well, once I had to break a strike in Oshawa, but we had to keep those assembly lines moving. What's good for General Motors is good for Ontario, I always say. I had the province's best interests at heart. Keeping me on as premier, don't you see. Well, I can tell you ..."

"Don't tell me much."

"Mitch. I was going to tell you about my kids."

"Another time. Mr. Heartburn."

"Hepburn. Five. I got five. All the same. Five darling little quintuplets."

"You have quintuplets?"

"Well, not me personally. Uh, I had to, er, appropriate them for their own safety. From the Dionnes."

"And enhance your reputation, such as it was?"

"Just a byproduct, my boy. See, this poor family up north had quintuplets, and they couldn't afford to keep them, so they were sorely tempted to allow their children to be exploited for commercial purposes. I made them wards of the Great Province of Ontario to protect them from undue harassment and exploitation."

"And they lived normal lives

happily ever after?"

"As near normal as I could make it."

"That's interesting, Mr. Hepburn, but we don't have much demand for quintuplet baby-sitters, King-bashers, or limo auctioneers. But listen, I'll see if Mr. Drew can find you a job in a liquor store, if you're really a Tory at heart."

The Legend of the House of Hepburn

CHAPTER ONE

AND it came to pass in the summer of 1943 that the King determined that he should test his popularity with the people.

2 Now this was a new King, who came to be known in time as Nixon the First, of no kinship nor kingship to Nixon the Noxious, ruler of the Americas in later years.

3 This new King had not ascended to his throne through the electoral process, but through the traditional laying on of hands within the royal Liberal family.

4 As was the custom in those times, the King would seek the favor of the Oracle of Ontario before testing the will of the people. And so, King Nixon struggled to the top of Hamilton Mountain to seek wisdom.

5 Verily, it was not the easy climb he had been led to expect. He pursued a rocky and dangerous path, narrow and clinging to the face of the precipice. And in one of these most constrained passages, on the face of the sheer cliff, the King was challenged by a dirty and shrunken and ragged man.

6 "Prithee, Your Majesty, go no further," said the man. "Thou seekest the oracle in vain. Return to thy throne and await thy fate."

7 "How know ye that I am King?" Nixon the First demanded. "Forsooth," said the old man, "no one but kings pass this way, in search of the truth and the blessing of the Oracle of Ontario."

8 "I tell thee, sire, there is no good news for thee atop the mountain. Thy family has cursed the people of this land with

the wretched reign of Mitch the Hepburn, and for that thee and all thy offspring shall be banished from the throne for years, for decades, for centuries, perhaps forever."

9 Now the King was much amused by this prophet. Had not the Liberal family enjoyed a free and noble reign? He pushed forward, and as he brushed past the ragged figure, the prophet stumbled and fell from the precipice, disappearing into the smoggy gloom of Steeltown below.

CHAPTER TWO

NOW the King was somewhat saddened by the loss of one of his constituents. A vote is verily a vote. But yea and behold, he did press on until he reached the very pinnacle of Hamilton Mountain.

2 And there, as it is written in the Holy Road Map of the Province of Ontario, he did find a limestone cave. And at the back of the sacred cavern, he beheld the fabled flame of truth and virtue kindled by yesterday's *Globe and Mail*. The Oracle sat beyond the flame, which was verily a

converted blast furnace. And the visage of the Oracle was obscured by smoke and gases.

3 "O most noble Oracle!" the King toadied, "I am Nixon, to be known someday as Nixon the First, and of no kinship nor kingship to Nixon the Noxious, a future ruler of the Americas. I come to seek your prophecy and your blessing, for I am about to test my popularity amongst my people."

4 The Oracle responded, "O King, test not. Thy family has visited upon the people of this land the wretched reign of Mitch the Hepburn. Thou shalt pay for the sin of the Mitch, and if thou test thy popularity thou shalt lose thy throne."

5 The King was deeply distressed. These were the very words uttered by the prophet who had fallen from the face of the cliff. "I have no choice!" the King cried. "The people demand I test my popularity, and I must comply lest I have my throne wrested from me."

6 The Oracle sighed. "That's tough, fella. Mitch the Hepburn has fouled thy palatial nest, and now thou must learn to live in humble exile."

7 Falling to his knees, the King begged to know more. "How long shall I be in exile? What shall I do to regain thy favor?"

8 Behind the smoke and gases, the Oracle shrugged. "I cannot tell you, for if I say a year, thou wilt do nothing about it for eleven months. If I say five years, thou wilt do nothing about it for four years. If I say ten years, thou wilt do nothing about it for nine. For such is the way of politics."

9 "And so I say unto thee, go forth and be good always. When thy time is right, I shall call thee. Calleth not me."

10 At that moment, the flame of truth and virtue began to flicker and wane, and before it expired unto death, the King caught a small glimpse of the visage of the Oracle. And it was indeed the prophet whom he had accidentally pushed to his death upon the mountain.

11 And the King reflected on the prophet, who had said he would be in exile "for years, for decades, for centuries, maybe forever." And the King was sore afraid.

CHAPTER THREE

AND lo! The Oracle *was* prophetic! King Nixon the First was dethroned by his people in the summer of 1943. A young prince, called George of Drew, founded the House of Torrey. And it was to be a House of long lineage.

2 King Nixon, unable to assail George of Drew, quit his household in the following year, and Mitch the Hepburn, though long of tooth, regained his place at the head of the family.

3 And so it came to pass, in the year 1945, Mitch the Hepburn ascended the Mountain to seek the truth from the Oracle.

4 "Verily, verily, I say unto thee," the Oracle began, "thou art still a man whose reign hath curst this land for many years."

5 But Mitch the Hepburn was contrite. "I have changed, O Oracle!" he cried. "If thou wouldst deliver this land from the clutches of mine enemy, George of Drew, I shouldst make it the promised land which we Liberals have so often promised, though never produced."

6 "Get thee below!" shrieked the Oracle. "George of Drew art a man of vision!

Thou art nought but a power-lusting Liberal!"

7 And so it was that in the summer of 1945, the Oracle was once more proven prophetic. George of Drew was re-crowned King of the land of Ontario.

CHAPTER FOUR

MITCH the Hepburn annoyed the Oracle no more. A younger prince, Farquhar, The Oliver, assumed his role as head of the Liberal family.

2 And as it had been written in the scriptures of the ancient prohibition, bad medicine came again to those who dare dally with the high spirit of evil drink.

3 George of Drew saw that the laws of alcohol of Ontario were perverse. And so he did attempt to change them to permit the consumption of hard and hearty liquor in the licensed drinking halls of the land.

4 Farquhar, The Oliver, was perplexed by what this meant. As had his fore-fathers before him, he ascended the face of the Hamilton Mountain to seek the wisdom of the Oracle.

5 "What ho!" he cried, upon seeing the Oracle crouched behind his boiling cru-cible of fermenting grain mash. "Hast thou cast thy lot with George of Drew's licentious ways?"

6. The Oracle was enraged. "Thou up-start Liberal! Thou wouldst deny thy people the pleasure of a tasty drink, but thou wouldst do the same if thou wert George of Drew."

7 "Never mind all that," taunted Far-quhar, The Oliver, who was by now quite convinced that the Oracle was nought but a Torrey smokescreen. "Dost thou foresee that liquor shall limit George of Drew's sharp vision?"

8 "Aye," said the Oracle. "The people shall reject George of Drew, but thou shalt not be King."

9 Farquhar, The Oliver, was puzzled. If George of Drew should not be King, then why not he?

10 And lo, the Oracle foretold the truth. George of Drew was barred from the palace of Queen's Park by a people's coup, but Farquhar, The Oliver, was forced to sit in isolation while yet an-other Torrey prince ascended to the throne.

CHAPTER FIVE

THIS newest Torrey ruler, Thomas of Kennedy, was not a prince at all, but merely a janitor, a caretaker, so it was said, who dusted the throne daily until a worthy successor could be found.

2 And lo! A noble prince named Les, the Early Frost, ascended to the throne. He was to enjoy a long and favorable reign, unscathed by a succession of Liberals who would usurp his throne.

3 Time and again, the Oracle would rebuff these Liberals in their pilgrimages to the pinnacle of Hamilton Mountain.

4 "Thou art still to pay for the sins of the Mitch," the Oracle told Walter, Thom's son, in the year 1951. "The dreams of George of Drew have not yet been fulfilled."

5 "Begone!" The Oracle screamed at Farquhar, The Oliver, who had one more kick at the veritable can in 1955. "This is the era of the Highway, the concrete fibres by which Les, the Early Frost, shall bind this land together."

6 "Get off my Mountain," the Oracle ordered John of Wintermeyer, a brash

and fervent idealist who would seize the power from the Torreys. "Les, the Early Frost, hath laid his iron fist upon this land, and thou shalt never sit thy bottom upon the throne of power."

CHAPTER SIX

BUT yea and verily, Les, the Early Frost, did not reign forever. He abdicated his throne to Prince John, House of Robarts.

2 Once more John of Wintermeyer struggled up that beaten path to the height of Hamilton Mountain. "Hey, Oracle," he shouted in blind frustration. "What do you say now? Les, the Early Frost, has taken his departure and I, John of Wintermeyer, am his most natural successor. Who is this dullard Londoner, this John, House of Robarts."

3 Again, the Oracle was enraged. "Two decades have passed since I hath told thy ancester, King Nixon, that thy family shall be banished from the throne for many years. Did I not tell him, as I tell thee now, that I shall call thee when thy time has come? Calleth not on me again."

4 Nor did John of Wintermeyer ever call upon the Oracle again. In a fierce and mighty battle in the year 1963, his army was humbled by the forces of John, House of Robarts.

5 And John of Wintermeyer was succeeded by Andrew, of the House of Thompson, who had but a short and tragic reign. In ascending to the top of the Mount called Hamilton, he ran afoul of the high priest, Charles of the Temple. Upon indulging in the ceremonial wine, Andrew, of the House of Thompson, did run his donkey-cart off the cliff and plunged to a most ignoble end.

CHAPTER SEVEN

AND it came to pass that in the year 1967, a new Liberal prince was picking his way up that well-trod path.

2 And as he crossed a cliff face, at that same constrained passage where King Nixon had confronted a prophet so many years before, a dirty and ragged and shrunken old man appeared.

3 "Do I not know thee?" asked the old man. "Hast thou not been here before? Art thou not Nixon?"

4 Whereupon the prince answered, "I don't know. No, and yes. I know not who thou art, I have not been here before, but verily, I am Nixon."

5 The old man drew back in horror. "King Nixon. Thou threw me from this very spot to my death many years ago. You seek the Oracle again, and yet I tell thee, there is no good news for thee atop the mountain."

6 "I know thee not," insisted the prince. "Perchance thou confuseth me with my father, Nixon the First, of no relationship to Nixon the Noxious, ruler of the Americas."

7 Now Nixon, like his father, was much amused by this prophet. And like his father before him, he sought to push on in his haste to reach the summit. And again, the prophet stumbled and fell from the precipice into the hazy gloom below.

8 Nixon the Second was sore afraid. This was indeed an unwelcome omen. And when he reached the limestone cavern of the Oracle, he beheld to his horror the same old man sitting behind the bubbling cauldron of half-baked Liberal campaigns.

9 "I warned thee not to come, as I

warned thy father," shrieked the Oracle. "But thou wouldst seek the truth, so thou shalt have it. Three times thou shalt ride to battle against the Torrey forces, and three times thou shalt be defeated. On the third time, thou shalt have victory within thy grasp, and thou shalt deny it."

10 Nixon the Second was aghast. If this were true, he had indeed picked himself a rocky row to hoe.

CHAPTER EIGHT

TOO quickly, Nixon the Second felt the sting of the Oracle's truth.

2 In a mighty dust-up in the fall of 1967, when all the people of the land were basking in the glory of a hundred years of nationhood, the army of John, House of Robarts, easily put to flight the ill-equipped foot-soldiers of Nixon the Second.

3 But John, House of Robarts, was to quit the throne in the year 1971. And in his place sat another stalwart Torrey, William the Davis, of the House of Brampton.

4 Nixon the Second held no fear of Davis. For was not the spirit of Trudeau upon the land, and were not the Torreys in full disarray everywhere?

5 But Nixon the Second had not counted on a vital development in military warfare. The Torreys, through much ingenuity, had invented a powerful weapon called the Big Blue Machine. In the autumn of 1971 the terrible weapon rolled over the archers and infantrymen of Nixon the Second.

6 In the following years, there was much trouble in the royal household of William the Davis. A number of black sheep were discovered in the royal kitchen, to be released out the back gate and slaughtered among the people.

7 And when another survey of popularity was due in the fall of 1975, Nixon the Second was extremely pleased. William the Davis was not a favorite among the people. But the people demanded that the two men appear together, so that they might judge which was more fit to rule. And Nixon ridiculed Davis, which sorely tried the patience of the people. And they chose William the Davis as their King once more.

8 And Nixon the Second remembered the prophecy that on the third time he should deny victory. And he said unto himself, "Oh damn!"

CHAPTER NINE

MORE time passeth, and soon the Liberals decideth that they needed a new face to put before the people.

2 And verily, in time yet another prince presenteth himself before the Oracle in the cavern on the Mountain.

3 "I do not believeth what I see," said the Oracle. "Art thou not a Jewish shrink from Montreal? And thou wouldst become King of Ontario? Hast thy family lost its marbles? Begone!"

4 And so Smith, House of Stewart, was thrashed in 1977, and again in 1981.

5 Which is to say, another Liberal prince, Peter the son, seeks the truth upon the mountain. And verily, the Oracle hath no answers, for the Oracle is the will of the people, and the people will what the people will, depending on the weather of the day and the strength of the Torrey advertising campaign.

6 So it is written, according to the Legend of the House of Hepburn.

PART IV

The Age of the Amethyst

In the post-war era and into the modern day, Ontario truly has been basking in glory. The province has enjoyed the fruits of its labor, becoming—like the official gem itself—an object sitting around and looking pretty. Neighbors to the east and neighbors to the west may threaten to start their own banana republics, but Ontario sits still and stolid in the middle of the country, as Canadian as the amethyst and as emotional as yesterday's gruel.

Ontario As She Be:
Lessons in Geography

LESSON 1: The Southeastern Border

The eastern border of Ontario with Quebec, way down there past Cornwall, is shaped like this: <

Natural justice says the Ontario border should follow the Ottawa River down to the St. Lawrence River near Montreal, to form an angle like this: > This would have been a lot neater on the maps. It also would have prevented a lot of highway accidents, since Ontario Provincial Police report that an unusual number of east-bound cars on the Macdonald-Cartier Freeway plunge off the highway just east of Cornwall.

Intensive research by the Ontario Ministry of Transportation and Excommunications has revealed that most of these accidents involve married couples who are making their first trip to Quebec.

It has been determined through surveys guaranteeing anonymity that the accident occurred when the passenger, most often the wife, looked at the road map and said, "Dear, why does Quebec have a piece of Ontario?"

To which the driver, usually the husband, would say, "Dear, Quebec does not have a piece of Ontario," to which in reply she would say, "Yes, dear, look at this."

Provincial police report that many drivers involved in accidents in the Cornwall area are found with road maps wrapped around their heads.

The historical fact is that Quebec was given this piece of Ontario by Upper Canada puritans as a buffer zone to protect themselves from the sins of Montreal.

In spite of that, the sins of Montreal were visited upon them in the long history of the Canadiens thrashing the Leafs at the Maple Leaf Mint.

LESSON 2: The Northwestern Border

The northwestern border of Ontario goes straight up from the American border for a piece, then bends at an angle, approximately like this: /

Nobody knows quite why this is, except that it complicates things for children in geography contests.

According to one legend, the Government of Ontario wanted to extend it straight up forever or until it reached Santa Claus' house, whichever came first.

The Government of Canada wanted to bend it at right angles at the elbow, barring rheumatism, to direct it eastwards to the Quebec border. It demanded the right to declare that all mineral resources beyond that latitude were "Mine, all mine."

After three royal commissions, a parliamentary study, and reference to the Privy Council, it was agreed that the spirit of compromise should prevail and that the border should trail off at an angle, like this: / until it ran out of land.

In this way, Ontario was spared the embarrassment of being saddled with places like Gillam and Bird in Manitoba. These burgeoning metropolises would have been in Northwestern Ontario today if the border had been in a straight line north, which is what the Creator intended in the first place.

However, this unnatural angling of the border deprived Ontario of the bustling port of Churchill. In at least one secret correspondence with Gabriel Dumont, Louis Riel confessed that he was not fighting for self-government, but to preserve the port of Churchill for the future province of Manitoba.

"I do not seek gain for my part," he wrote, "I merely seek grain for my port."

Today, the residents of Moosonee are grateful for the Canadian compromise. If Ontario had retained the port of Churchill, it is extremely doubtful that Moosonee would have developed into a major transhipment point for Moose Factory.

To this day schoolchildren in Manitoba are taught that Ontario stole part of their heritage. That is a lie, of course, but if they want it back they have to take Grassy Narrows as is—no extra charge for the mercury deposits.

LESSON 3: The Northeastern Border

For many years, the Ontario Ministry of Mines and Maps has been plagued with letters and petitions about the northeastern border of Ontario.

Most amateur cartographers are enchanted with the manner in which the northeastern Ontario border wends its leisurely way northwestward from the St. Lawrence, up the Ottawa River to Mattawa, then turns lazily northwards towards Lake Timiskaming.

To that point, it behaves as all borders do, following the obvious geographic demarcation provided by the natural terrain. But at the northern end of Lake Timiskaming, the border develops a mind of its own and heads due north towards the pole.

This sudden shift in character has dumbfounded cartographic sleuths for decades.

The truth is, the border of Ontario could easily have swung west at Mattawa and zipped straight across Lake Nipissing to Georgian Bay. All of Northern Ontario could have been part of La Belle Province, or worse, Manitoba.

In the spring of 1879, survey crews from Quebec and Ontario fought hand-to-tripod combat all the way from Hawkesbury to New Liskeard. They were evenly matched teams, forcing each other to stick to their respective shores of the Ottawa. This was relatively easy, because neither crew had thought to bring a canoe.

At the head of Lake Timiskaming, they came face to face for the first time.

"Listen, my friend," said the chief of the French crew, "we are a long time from home. It is getting on to the fall, and nobody knows where we are. Nor do they care. We will make a deal. You give us all of the land north of lac Nipissing, and we will give you Penetanguishene."

The Ontario crew chief was astounded. "We already have Penetanguishene. If you give us everything east of Lake Timiskaming, we will give you back Penetanguishene, and throw in Windsor too."

The Quebec crew chief thought for a moment. "It is a deal I would make if I were in a bar in Montreal, but I am not. We have two options. We can continue from here in a straight line north and spend the winter in the snow. Or, we can do it the bureaucratic way. You claim all the land east of here, I will claim all the land west of here. We will file our reports. The dispute will go to Ottawa. They will dither for a few years, then draw a line straight north from here. It is a compromise. Believe me, *mon ami*, it always works. That is why we have had no trouble with the Labrador border."

Pit Stop

Colborne strode into his boss's office in the Ontario Ministry of Transportation, Communication, and General Movements of People and Livestock. He proudly laid a detailed document on Trenton's desk. "There. The ultimate contract for a Macdonald-Cartier Freeway Pit Stop."

Trenton frowned. "We'll see."

He began reading. "Uh-huh. Get the gas prices up top. 'Gasoline to be priced at a minimum of 10 cents per litre above the prevailing average rate.' Good, good. Their eyes will light up when they see the prospective profits."

Trenton moved on. "Let's see what you say about food. 'Sandwiches to be four days old, or equivalent.' How can they be equivalent?"

Colborne was ready. "Easy enough. Air Canada has developed a method of instantly aging sandwiches. It isn't patented, so we stole the idea from them. Basically, it involves passing exhaust gases from the service station through the refrigerated sandwich case. By noon, today's freshest sandwiches taste like they were grilled on the engine block of a Voyageur bus."

Trenton was stunned. "Incredible! I had no idea technology had advanced that far. Okay, what about soft drinks? 'All soft drinks shall maximize the recycling aspects of the Environment Act of Ontario to the best of the ability of the service division.' What does that mean?"

"Oh, they simply carbonate anti-freeze and other liquids drained out of cars in the service centre. If they heat it, they can serve it for coffee. It's all spelled out in detail in a little booklet we give the chef."

"And what qualifications shall the chef have?" Trenton asked. "Hmmm. 'Chef shall be able to read the little booklet from the Department of Transportation, Communication, and General Movements of People and Livestock'. That's all?"

Colborne said, "That's all. And that's not tough. We use a lot of pictures and symbols in the little booklet. Rads and hoses and cups, that sort of thing."

"What about staff?" Trenton asked. "Oh, yes, here it is. 'Staff to have an average age of 18, a maximum education of grade 6, an average IQ of 90, and an ability to display an utterly indifferent and bored attitude towards serving the public at all times.' At all times?"

Colborne didn't flinch. "There's a problem with permitting them to welcome some customers. If some people get the idea they're welcome at these service centres, they're apt to spread the word and then others will be griping that they didn't get better service. Experience has taught us that if the public is uniformly insulted, nobody ever expects too much."

Trenton was surprised. This lad really knew his stuff. "Now, then, what have you ordered about washrooms? 'Washrooms to be cleaned at least once a week.' Do you really think it's necessary to have a minimum?"

Colborne replied, "Afraid so. The Ministry of Health and Other Impediments to Big Profits threatened to close the places down if the washrooms weren't cleaned at least once a week. Don't worry. Those places can become the legendary pigsties in less than a week, particularly over a holiday weekend."

Trenton smiled. "You're pretty clever. I think you should change the wording so that it reads, 'Washrooms to be cleaned once a week, on the Monday preceding a holiday weekend.' That will ensure that the washrooms are at their absolute filthiest by the holiday."

Colborne quickly agreed. "Excellent idea. I think we've got the perfect contract."

Trenton shook his head. "Never, my boy. Next year, we're going to play recordings of speeches by the minister in the 401 restaurants. If we don't maintain a high degree of insulting behavior, our customers will just keep coming back for more."

Fleesdale Ruins the Game

"I bet," said Owl, rolling his eyes behind his glasses, the way he always did, "old man Pershey doesn't make it."

Owl could be right. Owl was regarded as the wisest of our quartet of twelve-year-olds. That's why we called him Owl. We weren't very original.

Pershey was the standard by which we measured history. We figured once Pershey went, the ceremony would be over. The four of us had grown up watching Pershey struggle up the hill every year, each year slower than the last, each year the sun becoming unbearably hotter, each year the flagstaff digging deeper into his belly, each year his aging, scraggly companions becoming fewer.

"Sure he will," Bick said. "Pete MacIntosh is weaker than him. Ol' Pete couldn't even carry his flag last year. He'll go first."

We chortled. It had been great fun last summer. Arthur Fleesdale was strutting up the hill, beating his big bass drum, when suddenly he toppled forward, directly into Herb Armstrong. For a moment, he lay draped over his drum, head almost touching the pavement in front, feet splayed on the road behind. Then he slowly slid off to the side. Freed of his body weight, the drum began bounding back down the hill.

Any one of us kids could have caught it on the bounce, but it wasn't heading for a bunch of kids. It mowed down the line of marchers behind, like a bowling ball in tenpins. George Harris was knocked out cold, Richard Afflass lost his false teeth, and Bobbie Cathcart broke his arm and a leg. I don't think he ever walked again. No, he didn't, because he spent the next eight months in a wheelchair until he died.

Well, it was a horror show. All these old men, lying there on the road amid their gold-fringed flags and broken eye-glasses, trying to maintain some dignity. Not that we cared much for them, but we were counting on a gradual attrition of the forces. If we were going to be deprived of this summer ritual, we would rather it happened naturally, than by a freak accident. All of us had bet on who would be last. This sort of thing could ruin the contest. I had chosen Pershey. Fortunately the drum missed him.

None of them was killed outright, except Arthur Fleesdale. But of course he died of a heart attack. That's what had started the whole thing.

Anyway, this summer a lot of the old men decided they didn't want to march. They would rather sit in the church and wait for the parade to arrive. In fact, there were only two who chose to make that long march up the hill, braving the hot July sun, risking the possibility of a windy day in which both flag and bearer would be whipped aside by a vagrant gust and tossed like tumbleweed into the ditch.

Those two, Peter MacIntosh and Harold Pershey, were forming up now, taking their places in the centre of the road right in front of the Orange Hall. The annual church parade always started right in front of the Orange Hall. The march from Orange Hall to Anglican Church symbolized strength and unity within the village.

The horizontal distance from the Orange Hall to St. Mark's Anglican Church was about a half-mile. The vertical distance was maybe 100 feet. To a kid on a bicycle, it wasn't much. To an eighty-year-old man toting a flag and military regalia, it was a stiff climb, but not so stiff that they couldn't follow tradition halfway up, where the Catholic Church was located on the left side of the road. Now, the only reason the Catholic Church was not at the top of the hill was that the Anglicans got here first, and there was only one hill in town. Anyway, in years past there had been a reviewing stand for the marchers placed opposite the Catholic Church. I didn't realize until I was eight that when the marchers went "eyes right", it was so they could turn away from the Catholic Church.

MacIntosh and Pershey were ready now. Owl, Bick, Ken, and I picked up our bicycles, ready to follow. If one of them dropped, we wanted to be on the scene. We had placed bets years ago, and Owl and I were the only ones left in the pool. I wondered if Owl could be right. Pershey did look a little pale, but MacIntosh's palsy was getting the best of him already.

Pershey looked at MacIntosh. "If it's all the same with you, Pete, I'm going to stay here," he gasped. "I don't think I can make it."

MacIntosh slowly furled his flag. "Well, Pershey, you know the rules. Chickening out is as good as dying. Old Fleesdale scared a lot of people out, going the way he did, and that was hardly fair. But there was still you and I, and now you've given up. I win the bet we made in 19-Ought-7. I always knew I'd be the last Orangeman in Ontario."

He lifted his chin high, unfurled his flag so that it nearly draped to the roadway before him, and began his long and final march up the hill. And Pershey sank to his knees, weeping. We four turned away in embarrassment and slowly and silently rode our bikes home. All bets were off.

L'indépendance de King Kirkland

The North was tired of being shoved around, and in the summer of 1974, a little-known group of northern nationalists huddled in The Miner's Hoist, a dingy bar in Virginiatown. They were deliberately meeting near the Ontario-Quebec border, for they had smuggled in the notorious Quebec anarchist, Jean-Louis Bombeposte.

They wanted ideas on how to achieve independence from the dominant South. "De first t'ing you do," said Jean-Louis, "is get me some decent *bière*. What is dis 'Carling'? Okay, Molson. Now, I tell you somet'ing, *mes amis*."

The small band of would-be world statesmen hunched closer around the tiny beer parlor table. Elbows slipped and slid in slopped lager as they tried to catch Bombeposte's instructions.

"Okay, it is *très simple*. You get de dynamite from de mine. For you, *pas de problème*. You make *la bombe*, and you issue de statement of independence."

There was a silence. A tall and scrawny fellow, Chappy Hughes, finally sputtered, "Uh, a bomb? With dynamite? What would we do with that?"

Bombeposte stared at him. "What do you mean, what would you do wit' it? You mail it to de premier in Toronto. Of course, it will blow up in the mailbox, but he'll get de message."

Hughes said, "No, I don't think so. We had something a little less exciting in mind, like writing letters."

Bombeposte ordered another *bière*. "Ah, I should have brought my brother Emile. He was in Ireland for a while, and he learned how to make de letters that go poof."

"Poof?"

"Oui, les lettres très explosifs. Is dat what you want?"

Another gang member, King Kirkland, spoke up. "No, no, we mean we want to write real letters of protest, for the premier to read." Bombeposte said he didn't understand. "We want to send the premier a message," Kirkland explained.

"Ah, *oui*, dat's what I said," Bombeposte nodded enthusiastically. "You blow up a mailbox on Government Road in Kirkland Lake, and he'll get de message. You blow up a mailbox in Brampton, and he'll—how do you say it?—pant his shits."

King Kirkland looked around at the other members of this assembly. This fellow was extraordinarily dense. It might be a language problem, but he didn't think so. He tried again. "We want to send the premier a communiqué outlining our grievances."

"Ah, *oui, oui,* a communiqué" Bombeposte shouted. "Why didn't you say so! Okay. It is very important to choose a proper symbol to put on de communiqué. Symbols are everything. *Une autre bière*, please."

Tarzwell Kearns, another conspirator, said, "I'm a bit of an artist. What kind of symbol?"

"Oh, in Quebec we used a woodsman. You could use, maybe, a miner with a screw in his back. It is symbolic, *n'est-ce pas?*"

Kearns said, "I don't know. We're serious about this thing. A miner with a screw on his back sounds like something naughty from a sex shop."

Bombeposte frowned. "Not on his back, IN his back. Right d'ere. Okay, I was not finished. D'ere is more. Dis symbol is used with anot'er which you must choose very carefully. De kidnap victim."

Kirkland, Kearns, and Hughes shrank back from the table in horror. Only Latchford Haileybury maintained a cool detachment. She had spent some time studying the history of the birth of nations at the University of South Porcupine. And she knew that in the birth of every nation, a little pang must come.

"Tell me, Mr. Bombeposte, what sort of person makes a good kidnap victim?"

"Oh, one dat somebody would want to recover. You never steal anybody dat nobody wants."

"I understand. For instance?"

"F'rinstance, maybe de mayor of Kapuskasing. Well, maybe not. Okay, de mayor of North Bay."

"Mr. Bombeposte, those are our people. Why would we kidnap one of our own people?"

"We did in Quebec, but you *Anglais* are funny people. Okay, you take de first cabinet minister what comes north and shut him up in a mineshaft somewhere. Den you cut off his right ear and mail it to de premier. Mind you don't mail a bomb at the same time. And den you wait."

Haileybury said, "Suppose we get no reply. I would expect that. The government has never paid any attention to us. Why should it get upset about finding a dried ear in the mail?"

"*Oui, oui.* Okay, if you want to get de message t'rough dat de victim's life is in danger, you mail de whole head."

Kirkland reeled off into the corner and threw up. Kearns fainted. Hughes excused himself for the evening. Haileybury ordered two more beers and asked Bombeposte, "And if this fails?"

Bombeposte shrugged. "You could mail de body to Toronto piece by piece. But d'ere is always de danger dey would wait until dey had all de pieces and put de minister back together. And you would have not'ing."

"Okay, suppose we threaten to withhold the rest of the body until Toronto takes action. What should we demand?"

Bombeposte grinned. "Better *bière.* Cheaper gas. Longer days in winter. More television stations. Better pizza. Longer summers. Fewer bears. Fewer mosquitoes. Extra blankets. Isolation pay."

Haileybury was not smiling. "I am sorry," Bombeposte said. "I was trying to make joke. Dis is a serious matter. You demand your own National Arts Centre, your own television network, your own radio network, your own book publishers, your own movie studios. But most *important*, you ask for an economic union wit' de sout'."

Haileybury sensed that Bombeposte was not in tune with the north's needs. "No, no, we want economic independence so we can keep the wealth up here," she explained. "But we want the *Toronto Star*, and the *Globe and Mail*, and CBC and CTV, the Maple Leafs and Harlequin Romances and the Hamilton Tigercats. We love importing culture!"

Bombeposte smirked and grimaced, then finished his *bière.* "I must be going. It is a long way back to my home in Quebec. Listen, I must tell you, I do not t'ink you nort'erners are ready for independence. Until you want your own newspaper in Gowganda, your own television station in Matachewan and your own theatre in Englehart, you will be slaves to de sout'. Economics? What is economics? Economics is what you get from Ottawa. You can only forge your own identity on someone else's money, my friend. *Au revoir.* Call me when you understand *l'indépendance.*"

A Fifty Second Flashback

Ernie: Hi there! This is Ernie Pakistanis, welcoming you to another "Fifty Second Flashback". Tonight we're going to review the entire history of professional sport in Ontario, shove in six beer commercials, and wind up with an inane comment from my co-host, Peter Marsbars. How ya feeling tonight, Pete?

Pete: "Couldn't be better, Ernie, matter of fact ..."

Ernie: "Thanks. Right now, a word from our sponsor."

(Blue, blue, blue, blue. Fade to black.)

Ernie: "Pete, the recorded history of professional sport in Ontario began approximately—let me check my stats—300 years, 3 months, 2 weeks, 4 days, 15 hours, 7 minutes and 37.986750334 seconds B.B."

Pete: "I know, I know. Basketball is a relatively new game."

Ernie: "No, no, B.B. means Before Ballard."

Pete: "I knew that. I was just joking ..."

Ernie: "No time for humor in sports, Pete. We've only got fifty seconds. More in a moment, but first another swig from our sponsor."

(Blue, blue, blue, blue, blue, glug.)

Ernie: "Hi, we're back again. Samuel de Champlain recorded the first sighting of professional sport in what became Ontario. While portaging through central Ontario he stumbled upon a game between the Algonquin Viscounts and the Iroquois Dukes as they were battling for top spot in the six-team Unexplored Wildlands Lacrosse League."

Pete: "Did Ballard have a franchise?"

Ernie: "No, he bought one later. But Champlain was so intrigued by the game that he wanted to play, and this led to the first racial incident in North American Pro Sport. The Indians said he was too short, that his beard would interfere with the opponents' vision, and that his French would disrupt the game. It soon became clear to Champlain that they really wouldn't let him play because he was a white man."

Pete: "So what did he do?"

Ernie: "Thank you for the question. I'll tell you and our audience, right after quaffing this message from our sponsor."

(Blue, blue, bleu, uh, blew, er, ah . . .)

Ernie: "Back again, folks. Well, Pete, he breathed on them and gave them smallpox and they all died."

Pete: "Ha, ha, ha. That was definitely an off-side play."

Ernie: "Sure was. A few years later, a bunch of Greek sailors with nothing to do got some canoes and formed the first Argonaut Rowing Club in Toronto."

Pete: "I thought Champlain was French."

Ernie: "This is a new story. We've only got fifty seconds. Well, the Argonauts never won a race because the men kept skipping back to the shed where they stored the oars. It was also where the rowing groupies waited for them, and the Argonaut coach just couldn't keep his men out of the oar-house! Ha, ha, ha!"

Pete: "Ernie, canoes don't have oars. They have paddles."

Ernie: "Right, Pete. And now another welcome break from our sponsor."

(First there was blue and then there was light,
Try our new lager and get yourself tight.)

Ernie: "Okay, Pete, I'll explain the oar story later. We've still got a few seconds, so I'll tell you about the merger of professional sports. It began in 1947, when the Calgary Stampeders brought their horses into the Royal York and tried to breed a rodeo and a football game; specifically, the Stampede and the Grey Cup."

Pete: "What a match! You just can't say enough about those horses!"

Ernie: "You just did. Anyway, it didn't work out. The chuckwagons tore up too much turf rounding the goal posts, and the Society for the Prevention of Cruelty to Animals complained that the linemen were roughing the bulls deliberately, despite the 15-yard penalties. The bulls, being smarter, filed assault charges. But the matches continued until the first artificial turf was installed, and the chuckwagon cook burned a hole in the carpet making coffee. That ended them, in 1972."

Pete: "Where was Harold Ballard?"

Ernie: "He was trying to cross tiger-cats and maple leaves, but instead of Canadian tiger milk he got striped maple syrup. Tell you all about it in a minute, but first. . . ."

(A bubbly young brewer named Slew,
Away in a balloon did he flew.
He made a fast pass
At a simple sweet lass
Who couldn't tell real beer from blue.)

Ernie: "Back again for the final few seconds. Harold Ballard had a hockey team called the Toronto Maple Leafs, so he bought the Hamilton Tiger-Cats, and he used both teams as excuses to kick newspaper reporters out of Maple Leaf Gardens. Everybody loved Hal because if he wasn't around they'd have to write nasty stories about people they really liked. And that's all the time we have tonight, folks."

Pete: "We're supposed to be talking about pro sports. You forgot the Ottawa Rough Riders."

Ernie: "No I didn't. Good night."

Made in Ontario, Finally

Sex is not indigenous to Ontario. It was imported from abroad.

It was first spotted on an American sailing ship on Lake Erie in 1780, but fortunately the ship's doctor was able to cure the spots and prevent the spread of the disease.

But this was a sign of things to come. Despite their best efforts, The Authorities have been unable to prevent sex from infiltrating almost every aspect of Ontario society.

It has even (as of 1952) violated a furrow at the International Plowing Match.

An early report received by The Authorities in 1796 suggested that sex was surreptitiously imported by Frenchmen working out of the Virgin Islands. A commission was quickly established and dispatched to check out the Virgins. It soon returned.

"Horrible place," scowled the commission chairman. "No fun at all."

"Well now," exclaimed the governor-general, "in all the Virgins ..."

"Exactly!" roared the chairman. "They're all virgins. No fun at all!"

In 1808 Scotland Yard warned the detective-inspector of the Upper Canada Colonial Police that a shipment of sex was on its way from Liverpool, via Edinburgh, and the Outer Hebrides. The shipment turned out to be a boatload of steak and kidney pies, augmented by a year's supply of haggis for all of Glengarry County.

"Quite like the British to mistake steak and kidney pie for sex," snorted the detective-inspector of the UCCP. "They serve them both cold. Still, there's probably some kook around who knows some kinky tricks with haggis."

Immigrants from Germany were accused of importing sex in the late 1820s. It was apparently a musical variety. Landlords who rented rooms to these immigrants complained that loud tuba playing disturbed their sleep every night. The German immigrants, in turn, explained that the tuba playing was necessary to cover up the embarrassing squeaking and squealing of the inferior bedsprings provided by slum landlords.

Love-making with a tuba has never been pictured, let alone satisfactorily explained. A report in the *New Berlin Bratwurst* on May 29, 1828, said, "While Old-country Germans are expected to contribute to their new communities, some things must remain our ethnic secrets, such as how we can eat sauerkraut for breakfast daily, how we get big pigs into little sausage skins, and how we make whoopee and oom-pa-pa simultaneously." Nevertheless, The Authorities banned tubas in Upper Canada between 1828 and 1842, except for ceremonial purposes. While they had no proof that Germans were using tubas to promote sex, they assumed that men running around in leather pants must be up to no good behind closed doors.

Quebec was naturally regarded with suspicion as an illicit source of sex. After all, the Church advocated mass reproduction, right after mass itself, as a means of assuring a steady growth in the bingo trade. In later years reproduction was replaced with Xeroxation.

Protestants in Upper Canada simply refused to believe that so many women and so many men could be cloistered for life without some evil intent to subvert their part of the universe. Convents and monasteries were, therefore, regarded as fronts for Organized Sex. A group calling itself the Popular Orange Dominion Front for Church Chastity and Tuba-bashing, with its roots in left-over anti-German sentiment, enrolled three spies in 1848 in a co-ed Quebec monastery, Les Belles de Ste. Marie et les Frères des Mains.

Fourteen years later the three spies returned to Ontario, reporting that they had been unable to find even a vestige of sex anywhere within the monastery, but would like to return for another fourteen years of study.

The Popular Orange Dominion Front was dismayed by this report, reading between the lines that there was activity between the sheets. They set about to exact revenge, and eventually invented the drive-in theatre, which they exported to Quebec. It quickly replaced all forms of recreational bingo except the rhythm game.

In the 1860s, Canada was too busy giving birth to a country to worry much about sex. This momentary national preoccupation with another topic enabled the promoters of sex to gain a significant toe-hold. The toe-hold was an instant success, practised in even the most fashionable bedrooms on Toronto's Jarvis Street for the next decade.

No one is sure who should be credited with importing the toe-hold. One popular theory suggests it was the Greeks. Because Greek men usually had their hands full of passing female buttock, they had to invent some other form of fond embrace to grasp their beloveds.

Another theory holds the Yugoslavians responsible. This theory notes that communist Yugoslavians arrived in Canada without shoes, as they were soul-less, and thus were in the best position to utilize the toe-hold.

No matter. The result of the toe-hold was that The Authorities were sent reeling in their avowed war on sex. The Popular Orange Dominion Front for Church Chastity, Tuba-bashing and Segregated Bunks on the CPR, scrambled to secure control of a rapidly deteriorating morality standard.

It took out full-page advertisements in the daily press, proclaiming that the toe-hold would lead to blindness and a love of pomegranates. It convinced Anglican pulpit-pounders to pronounce the toe-hold a mental affliction which would lead to untold generations of children born with clubfeet and a desire to open a greengrocer's shop on Toronto's Danforth. It convinced its former foe, the Roman Catholic Church, to threaten excommunication for any of its flock found practising the toe-hold in a drive-in theatre.

The anti-sex campaign apparently worked. By 1902, a Gallup Poll reported that seventy-seven per cent of Canadians were tired of sex feet-first. Twelve per cent had no opinion on sex, and eleven per cent slammed the door on the pollster's peni ... er, pen.

A fast-frozen sex fad swept Ontario in the winter of 1910–11 after physics students at the Lindsay School of Irregular Anatomy carefully measured the bronze attachment on a statue in the town park of Michelangelo's famous David. They discovered that the attachment was a full quarter inch shorter on Jan. 14, 1911, at a temperature of -35 degrees Fahrenheit, than it had been on Aug. 23, 1910, at a temperature of 105 degrees Fahrenheit.

The students titled their report "An Exercise in Truncating the Essentials as a Result of Exposure to Cold Climate" subtitled, "It Won't Be Long Now."

The Lindsay League of Indecent Exposure raised enough money to buy a bronze loincloth for poor David. This was a health measure. Doctors in Lindsay reported a marked increase in the incidence of frostbite of male attachments throughout February, 1911, as scientifically-minded couples experimented without the usual precautionary measures in public parks, one-horse sleighs, and unheated library lofts.

All this was blamed on the Italians. Lindsayites reckoned that if the Italians had clad David properly in the first place, none of their youth would have had their flowering manhood nipped in the bud.

Common sense quickly overcame curiosity, and this flirtation with sex soon died out. Ontario was then sexless for another few years until assembly-line sex was imported from the United States.

This form of sex was steered across the border from Detroit. Henry Ford moved the rumble seat inside the automobile, a blatantly sexual move which, coupled with the wanton excesses of the drive-in theatre, inevitably led to the creation of the Pill. Motherhood was the necessity of invention.

The Authorities were nearly defeated by this assault on moral rectitude, but not quite. The Society for the Neutering of Implicit Photography (SNIP) was conceived, although not in a rumble seat. It was born as the Ontario board of censors, founded on the concept that if ideas could be stopped from flowing into the brain, the brain would not pass on those ideas to other less inhibited parts of the body.

At about the same time, another band of social leaders formed the Commission of Really Trivial Culture (CRTC). These people weren't concerned so much about the inflow of foreign sex for sex's sake, as they were about the fact that it was of foreign origin.

These were the nationalist puritans. They argued that sex per se was not harmful, providing it was Canadian sex. Those from Toronto felt especially strongly that it should be Ontario sex, while complaining at the same time that there wasn't any. People from smaller centres, such as London and Sarnia, were afraid that the Torontonians meant CBC sex. And those in much smaller places, such as Havelock, Leamington, and Haileybury, went about their way and enjoyed what they could, whenever.

With the arrival of the 1970s and the Age of Enlightenment, sex was well-entrenched across the province. It had reached such proportions that the Government tried to figure out a way to make money on it, through taxes or licences. A private bill to create the Sexual Licence Board of Ontario was nearly passed into law, and would have been, except that even the Conservative government could not hire enough relatives to post inspectors in every bedroom.

So there it is: a sordid tale of debauchery, a story of Ontario's moral degeneracy, a saga of sex that is best left where it is best laid.

Thrashing on the Trilliums

MAY 20, 1982
"C" Court, Simcoe Centre, Haldimand County

Provincial Judge R. Howard Pluckett: "All right, all right, what've we got here? Henry Grabball LaFleur, you are charged with theft under $200, to wit, that on the fourth day of May, 1982, you did pick and carry off one white trillium from a public place. How do you plead?"

LaFleur: "Guilty, yer honor."

Pluckett: "Guilty? Just like that? What kind of a trial is this?"

LaFleur: "Yer honor, I've known since I was kneehigh to a daffodil that it was illegal to pick trilliums in Ontario. I just lost my head."

Pluckett: "All right, all right, give the clerk $20 and go. Next!"

Court clerk: "John Charles Upjohn and Mary Goode Hayroll."

Pluckett: "John Charles Upjohn and Mary Goode Hayroll, you are jointly charged that in an area known as Dobbins Woods on the first day of May, 1982, you did wilfully and with aforethought trample upon the trilliums. How do you plead?"

Upjohn and Hayroll: "Not guilty, your honor."

Pluckett: "Very well. Will the crown proceed?"

Crown attorney: "Yes, your honor. Calling Constable Stamen Petal."

The court clerk administered the oath and Petal identified himself to the court.

Crown attorney: "Const. Petal, what is your position?"

Petal: "Reasonably upright."

Crown attorney: "I mean, what do you do for a living?"

Petal: "I am on foot patrol with the Royal Ontario Trillium Brigade."

Crown attorney: "Specifically, what is your job?"

Petal: "I am assigned to patrol, on foot, the paths and roads through Dobbins Woods to enforce Ontario Regulation TR-1111-UM."

Crown attorney: "To what does that pertain?"

Petal: "It's a protection racket for trilliums. Nobody is allowed to touch leaf nor petal of the white ones."

Crown attorney: "What about the pink and red ones?"

Petal: "Oh, we don't worry about those. They're Commie trilliums."

Crown attorney: "On the day in question, what did you see?"

Petal: "I was patrolling through Dobbins Woods and I came across a man and a woman among the trilliums."

Crown attorney: "Could you identify these people?"

Petal: "Yes, they are the accused."

Crown attorney: "Now, what were they doing among the trilliums?"

Petal: "Destroying them."

Crown attorney: "How?"

Petal: "They were crushing them."

Crown attorney: "They were walking on them?"

Petal: "No. They were lying on them."

Crown attorney: "Lying on them? They were sleeping on the trilliums?"

Petal: "If I may say so, sir, they were not sleeping. They were nude and thrashing about, actually. They had thrashed about quite a large area. It was an awful sight. I almost broke down and wept."

Crown attorney: "Did you count the number of trilliums they had destroyed?"

Petal: "Several hundred, I should say. They had also uprooted four pines and a maple."

A large gasp echoed through the courtroom. Pluckett himself popped his eyes open from his nap.

Crown attorney: "Trees can be replaced. Several hundred trilliums, you say?"

Petal: "Well, I think so, but it was hard to separate the crushed trilliums from the mushed poison ivy."

Crown attorney: "Did you bring this poison ivy to their attention?"

Petal: "I didn't have to. They were already itching to get out of there."

Crown attorney: "Did you inform them of their rights?"

Petal: "I did, although under Ontario Regulation TR-1111-UM, people don't have many rights. None, as a matter of fact. A police officer is entitled to shoot trillium mashers on sight."

Crown attorney: "That's all, your honor."

Pluckett: "My word, you two have gotten yourselves into an awful mess. Thrashing about naked on a bed of trilliums. What have you to say for yourselves?"

Hayroll: "I wish we'd checked for poison ivy."

Pluckett: "No remorse for crushing the trilliums, I see. You have set a terrible example for the public. If word of this escapade gets out, somebody will want to make a movie of it. 'Tryst on a Trillium.' Then we'll have to bring in our censor board, and before it's over this will have cost the province thousands of dollars, not to mention several hundred trilliums. I won't have it in my court. Seven years each!"

Hayroll: "Seven years!"

Upjohn: "Prison?"

Pluckett: "No, no, no! Seven years duty on the censor board. You people really have an eye for Ontario's erotic pleasures."

The Cult of the Silver Shears

In a dark and secret garret, high in the draughty stone towers of Queen's Park, a small band of mute, shrouded, and tight-lipped citizens gathered silently for another powerful rite of exorcism.

As they filed into the dank and musty room, each rushed quickly to a window. Shades were pulled, drapes were drawn, and only when the last glimpse of the outside world had been obliterated was a small candle lit and placed in the middle of the conference table.

A grim-faced matron, her sour, pinched features revolting and yet at the same time oddly repulsive, assumed command.

"Ladies and gentlemen, and you are ladies and gentlemen for otherwise you would not be here, we are facing a most formidable and appalling task. We have been chosen because we are believed to be resistant to the forces of evil which can infest and twist weaker minds, but we are not invulnerable. There will be casualties. And yet, we must be undaunted in our struggle to rid this great province of Ontario of the evil before us."

Around the table, six hooded figures nodded in impatient agreement. The high priestess of the exorcism leaned forward and, cupping a talon around the lone candle, squashed the life from the only source of light. In the darkness, the hooded figures began whispering and muttering. Slowly the murmuring blended into a chant, and soon the chamber echoed with the magic chorus.

The hooded figures, lusting for action, shouted out the fearful incantation, "Cut, cut, cut!" and pounded their ceremonial silver scissors on the table. Suddenly, above their heads, a spear of brilliant light shot out from a rectangular hole in the wall, and opposite them, a square of light splashed across a beaded screen. Darkness was banished and the hooded citizens covered their eyes with jewel-clad fingers.

But not entirely. For this was crucial to the rite of exorcism. Through trembling fingers, they were forced by bond of ritual to view the awful frescos upon the wall, to watch the devil himself create images which man was never meant to see, to deny the devil his moment of evil glory by hollering "Cut!" at the precise moment that the King of Hades was about to proclaim victory.

Another session of the Ontario Censor Board was beginning.

The rite proceeded. Within a moment, all was chaos. Two of the figures had turned their faces from the screen. Three were chuckling. One was yelling "Cut!" every fifteen seconds. Two went out for popcorn. The high priestess stabbed her diamond-studded scissors into the table and shrieked for order. She snapped her fingers and the images on the silver screen disappeared. She relit the candle and glared around the table.

"Ladies and gentlemen, we must come to some agreement on the invocation of the command to 'Cut!' We can only do this if we agree in advance, and I sense there is a deep rift among us over what we do when we see the naughty bits."

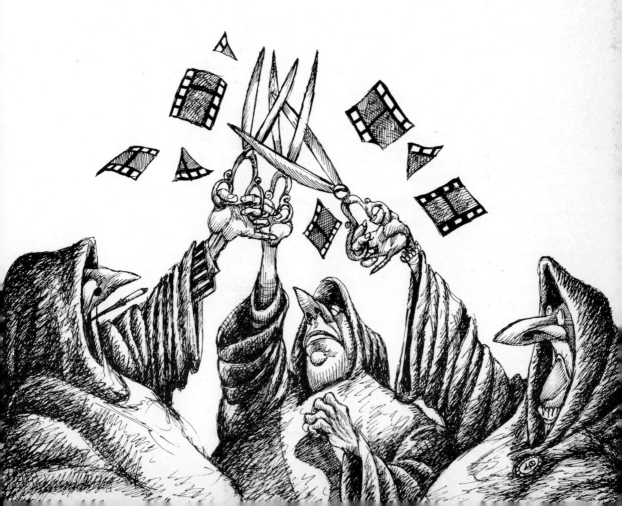

A small balding man, a liquor salesman, the blade of his scissors already warped in battle, asked, "Which naughty bits are we talking about?"

The priestess huffed, "Didn't you read the manual before you came here? The naughty bits are all spelled out in there."

The little man shrugged and hung his head. "I didn't get my job because I can spell, I got it because I know good booze. I'm not sure what's naughty, so I was cutting everything. Back where I come from, no decent young man ever thought to gaze on naked female clavicles. So I cut them out of *Knaughty Knight in Kenora.*"

The priestess snorted. "Clavicles are not on the list of naughty bits."

A middle-aged woman, a luggage clerk at Simpsons, peered from beneath her Naugahyde hood and said, "I took out all the moles in *Temiskaming Tryst.* Blackflies, too."

The priestess glanced at her with disgust and loathing. "Moles aren't naughty bits."

"Well, they are where I saw them," the woman insisted.

The two men who had gone for popcorn, one a car dealer and the other an American tourist in town for the weekend, returned to the room. "Hey," said the tourist. "What happened to *Oshawa Olga and the Ogre?* We were just getting to where she fondles the nuts on the assembly line."

"Yeah," leered the car dealer. "I really liked the way Olga was polishing her hub caps."

The priestess screeched. "How did you two get in here? This is a sacred rite. You have profaned it. You, you tourist, you're probably from Buffalo, or worse, Ogdensburg. And you, a car dealer, what do you know about art? Get out, get out!!" She snatched up her silver scissors and hurled them at the tourist. One blade caught him between the Instamatic and the travellers cheques, neatly severing his pack of Cabbagetown postcards.

The hooded bishop on the board, silent until then, spoke up. "My dear, we mustn't get overwrought. The premier doesn't really care how much we slice up films for Ontario theatres, but we must never, never discourage the tourists. That truly is a naughty bit of work."

Strike Up the Bland

When the Bicentennial Licence Plate Slogan Committee last met, Orville E. Tibbs, the mayor of Haliburton Corners, began sorting through the finalists in the slogan contest.

"An entry from East Hamilton," he shouted. " 'Trilliums Triumph Together'. It's sort of a union solidarity slogan for Ontario."

The other judges raised their scorecards. 4.5, 3.2, 1.2, 9.9. "That's my hometown," shrugged 9.9, the East Hamilton judge.

"This is an entry from Pollution Probe. 'Let's take the Die out of Dioxin.' That'll catch the eye of the environmentalists." 6.2, 4.3, 2.2, 8.9. "You gotta admit it's gotta ring," sniffed the East Hamilton judge.

"This has possibilities," said Tibbs. " 'Provincially yours!' " 3.5, 1.1, 2.3, 9.6. "Sounds okey-dokey to me," said the East Hamilton judge.

"Aha! Something in Latin. 'A frog usque a Winnipog'." 6.6, 4.3, 2.3, 9.7. "It rhymes! I love it!" exclaimed the East Hamilton judge.

"Okay, try this unity slogan. 'Let's all bland together.' " 7.5, 4.6, 2.9, 9.9. "Beautiful," said the East Hamilton judge. "It's so . . . so Ontario. Or should I say, it's so-so Ontario."

Tibbs threw the rest of the entries into the waste basket. "We ain't gonna do better than that," he chortled. "Let's go out and celebrate. The first round of pablum's on me."

A Bicentennial Game

RULES

1. Use board from any game. Monopoly is ideal, Trivial Pursuit suitable, and Parcheesi, Chess, or Chinese Checkers will do in a pinch. A euchre deck is inappropriate.

2. Object of game is to move as many times as possible without being seen.

3. Stealth is paramount. **If any other player detects your move, you take the game and go home.**

4. Moves are determined by dividing your OHIP code into Wintario ticket numbers. The resulting number is called a Trillium. The more Wintario tickets you buy, the more Trilliums you have to make secret moves to accomplish nothing.

5. Only the last two digits in the number can be used to calculate your Trillium. If your Wintario number divided by your OHIP code is 54381, your Trillium is 81. (No! No! You don't win a lottery prize! This is only a silly game!)

6. If your Trillium is higher than 20, you cannot play. Buy another Wintario ticket. This rule is sponsored by the Government of Ontario.

7. Here is what you do with your Trilliums. Each Trillium has a different value, allowing you to go here, there, and anywhere in Ontario to do nothing. For instance, a 25 Trillium allows you to tour Sarnia, all expenses paid.

TRILLIUM GUIDE

10–Visit the CN Tower and look up. Stay as long as you want. If a crowd gathers, **you lose**.

11–Ride to the top of the CN Tower and look down. Take your time. If anyone takes your picture, **you lose**.

12–Visit Niagara Falls. Watch the Niagara fall. If a television news crew gets a shot of you falling in, **you lose**.

13–Lie in the sun in a bathing suit at Wasaga Beach. If anyone points out that this is strange behavior in February, **you lose**.

14–Write to Ontario Government praising food on Tobermory ferry

Chicheemaun. If letter is published in tourist guidebook, **you lose**.

15–Drive through cornfields of Chatham Country. If local radio station interviews you on "Man in the Green" show, **you lose**.

16–Drive five times around Holland Marsh. If anyone asks whether you remember Hurricane Hazel and the Great Flood, **you lose**.

17–Visit Ottawa and talk to local residents. If anyone says, "I am not a civil servant," **you lose**.

18–Watch Queen's annual Christmas message. If neighbor phones up to ask if you watched The Queen, **you lose**.

19–Visit Pearson International Airport. Ask for directions to downtown Pearson. If anyone tells you that you are still in Toronto, **you lose**.

20–Visit Sarnia. If anyone asks why, **you lose**.

Remember: No matter how often you lose, success is just around the corner if you buy more lottery tickets.

CAUTION: Dead people don't have OHIP numbers.
Game ends upon death of any player.

Incroyable!
Magnifique!
Stupide!

C'est un jour très beau à Paris. François et Guillaume boivent du vin dans leur bistro favori, Le Café du Weekend Perdu. Ils ont bu trop du vin importé de St. Catharines et ils parlent de la sexe et de la religion et de la sexe et de la nuclear war et de la sexe. Maintenant ils discutent de la politique d'Ontario.

François: "*Mon Dieu*, you would not believe what I have learned about Canada. Every month, my cousin Roch who lives in Ontario sends me a letter. *Et, mon ami*, I get so depressed. The politicians, they talk of the French but they do of the English."

Guillaume: "*Au, oui, oui.* That is a very good description, I think. *C'est très bon! C'est magnifique!* Tell me, *mon ami*, what does it mean, to talk of the French and do of the English?"

François: "In Canada, such a crazy country, they spend all of their time and half the national product *très* gross worrying about the bilingualism. *Incroyable!* My cousin Roch, he says he could be a millionaire if he could find a market for bilingual hot air."

Guillaume: "This Canada, is it bilingual?"

François: "Yes, here and there. Here but not there."

Guillaume: "I think I will pour some more wine before I pursue this further. It is, but it is not. How is that?"

François: "It is if you are in an airport, but not if you are in a bus station. It is if you are in a police station where the policemen wear a yellow stripe on their pants, but it is not if you are in a police station where they do not."

Guillaume: "François, my old and tired brain is somewhat fuzzy with the wine of many years. I think it is that you are having the fun with me, is it not?"

François: "*Non, non. C'est vrai.* It is a matter of the provinces. It is bilingual in New Brunswick but not in Ontario."

Guillaume: "Ontario is not bilingual. Where is Ottawa?"

François: "In Ontario."

Guillaume: "But it is the capital. Is it not bilingual?"

François: "It is."

Guillaume: "I am sorry, *mon ami*, but I am having trouble with the logic of this. Perhaps there is no logic. Ontario is not bilingual but Ottawa is, although Ottawa is in Ontario. Why is not Ontario bilingual?"

François: "Roch says it is because of the metric road signs and the corn flakes."

Guillaume: "Please, you are going too fast for me, especially before my corn flakes. *Nous avons bu trop du vin; je ne mange pas des flocons de Kellogg's.* I do not understand."

François: "Roch says the anglos are afraid it will be forced down their throats."

Guillaume: "Where else would you put corn flakes? François, we have known each other a long time. Sometimes I think Roch must be having fun with you, and you do not know it. Remember when he told you the government of Ontario was something called Progressive Conservative?"

François: "Impossible, but true."

Guillaume: "*Non, non, pas possible.* How can a government be progressive and conservative at the once? *Mon Dieu!* If that were true, it would have everything both ways on every issue. People would see through that, and throw it out of office. Is this a new government?"

François: "Roch says it has been in power for more than forty years."

Guillaume: "There! You see? It is impossible for any government to have been in power for forty years, except in Russia. Do not be so alarmed by what your cousin Roch tells you. I think he makes it up. I am surprised he has not tried to make you believe that the country was run by a Frenchman in spite of all the anglos."

François: "Guillaume, have you been reading my mail? That is exactly what he said."

Guillaume: "*Ah, incroyable!* And you believed him? François, I thought that I was the gullible one. Ha, ha! They booted out our beloved Charles de Gaulle; they would never elect a Frenchman as leader. Sometimes I think you are always drinking too much wine."

PART V

The Age of the Elephant

Elephants enjoy both longevity and quick recall of their heritage. And so it will be with no regrets whatever that the cabinet will mark the Conservatives' 100th anniversary in power by selecting the elephant as Ontario's official beast. This will be foretold by the Oracle of Hamilton Mountain for anyone who dares climb the treacherous route to his lair. But is the elephant a wholly Canadian beast, or is it an American import? Only the Oracle knows for sure.

Ho-Hum, Another Century

JUNE 30, 2084
The Premier's Press Conference
Queen's Park

Premier Margaret Melita (Drips) Mercouri: "It's 2084, Ontario is 300 years old, women have been running the place for 50 years, and I say it's a helluva lot better. Any questions?"

Creighton Hondrich, *Metro Daily Sunstar:* "When are you going to solve the dioxin problem?"

Premier Drips: "I was just about to announce another commission to study the problem. Now, nobody should worry. It's true that the water in Lake Ontario will eat the feathers right off a wayward duck, but we're not sure whether that's caused by chemicals or acid rain. But let me assure you, dioxin is not swimming up the Humber."

Abu hm'n Dhabi Zgynmskyngnrrskuscki, *Cultural Broadcasting Corp.:* "What is this year's plan to preserve Ontario farmland?"

Premier Mercouri: "I am very pleased to announce that this morning cabinet has approved the construction of a shopping centre on the last ten acres of arable farmland in South Cayuga Township. This completes the urban link between St. Catharines and Windsor. As you know, our policy states that land is best preserved beneath asphalt. Otherwise, it just washes away."

Claridge McHydro, *National Cornerstone Globe:* "The leader of the opposition New Libercrats says the price of the Darlington nuclear station is now $15 billion. Is that true?"

Premier Mercouri: "Of course not. This morning it hit $25 billion, but look at the jobs we're creating. And as you know, as long as Pickering Units One and Two are out of commission, we need Darlington."

Jacqueline Tennant, *Rogers Worldwide Cable:* "Will you be lifting rent controls this year?"

Premier Mercouri: "I think in all due fairness to everyone concerned we'll hold them at six per cent one more year until we see where the economy is going."

Betty Sinclair, CFRB: "Who gives you the most trouble?"

Premier Mercouri: "Metro Southont Chairman Paul Godfrey III. He sticks his chin into everything. Ever since I added Grey, Bruce, Huron, and Simcoe Counties to his Metro council, he's been unbearable. He wants the City of Muskoka too, but he's not going to get it."

Pierre Trueblood, *Globular TV:* "What has been Ontario's biggest achievement in the past century?"

Premier Mercouri: "Keeping the Conservatives in power. As my great-grandfather, William Grenville Davis, used to say after he retired, 'The first forty years were the toughest'."

APPENDIX I

The Ontario Book of Lists

The Origin of Place Names
All Over the Map

SUDBURY: An anglicization of "sud beurre". Early French-Canadian prospectors in the Sudbury region used to place their frozen butter on the south window sill so that it would soften in the sunshine. This prevented traumatic fracturing of toast. Soft butter became known as "sud beurre" or "south butter." English prospectors corrupted it to "sud burry" and hence, Sudbury.

OMEMEE: In honor of the region's first music teacher. Falsetto Sharp. Originally the town had been named Doraymefasolatido, but even the music teacher found it difficult to pronounce after an evening of opera at the local tavern. The original name was immortalized in the movie, *The Sound of Music.*

NOTTAWASAGA: A river named by Giovanni Immigranti, a New Canadian explorer who was searching for a famous bathing beach on Georgian Bay. In a celebrated argument with his wife on the banks of the Nottawasaga, Giovanni uttered his famous line, "I'ma notta knowa where I am, but I know this notta Wasaga."

HONEY HARBOR: A name naturally evolving from the night dumping of the honey buckets from American yachts anchored in the harbor. Canadian yachtsmen simply hung over the rail.

RENFREW: A corruption of "rain through". Early Polish settlers in the Ottawa Valley lived in cheap tents while they built their log cabins. Irish settlers, claiming the same land, sometimes riddled the tents with buckshot. This dampened the Poles enthusiasm as life became a puddle of rain through the roof.

LONG SAULT (Long Soo): In an early Indian war (1752) a Sioux warrior was captured and tortured on the rack. The British intended to wring some information out of him. During the ordeal the Indian, who was 5'1" when captured was stretched to 6'8". Originally named Short Cornwall, he was known for the rest of his life as Long Sioux.

SIOUX LOOKOUT: Because of his extraordinarily long arms, Long Sioux (see Long Sault) was in great demand by pioneer basketball teams. Unfortunately, his long neck also placed his head above the rim. "Sioux!

Lookout!" was often cried by his teammates during a game whenever he rushed under the basket. He died when he accidentally beheaded himself during a championship game between Kenora and Wawa.

MACDONALD-CARTIER FREEWAY: Named after highway surveyors John Alexander "Sureshot" Macdonald and Jacques Cartier. Macdonald started from Windsor, Cartier from Montreal. They were surveying a two-lane highway, but in the thick undergrowth of the early Ontario wilderness they missed each and kept on going. Soon they had parallel road allowances laid out between the two cities. The Ontario Government to this day has not figured out why construction costs were exactly double the original estimate.

NIPISSING: Nothing to do with a Japanese immigrant relieving himself in a snowbank. Named after an East Indian restaurateur, Abjeen Fahred Singh. He had a passionate desire to bite the earlobes of his female customers, usually between the papadoms and the curried goat. He quickly earned the nickname "Nippy Singh" and gained many amorous admirers, some of them women.

NORTH BAY: Named for its location on the east end of Lake Nippy Singh.

BOBCAYGEON: Founded by Roberta Catphish, Miss Cajun Queen of Louisiana, 1845. Shortened by prudish councillors to Bobcaygeon in the 1890s. It was her dream to open a New Orleans style cabaret and whorehouse in the Haliburton region. Residents of the area, some of whom are descendants of Miss Catphish's pioneer group, dispute this fact.

BANNOCKBURN: A roadside restaurant, originally "You-stupid-ass-you've-charcoaled-the-goddamn-toast-again!"

KEMPTVILLE: The only legitimate usage of the positive form of the word "unkempt." Actually, a mispelling. The village was originally the country dwelling-place of mistresses of high-placed bureaucrats in Ottawa. Anyone whose lunch-hours stretched beyond the traditional three hours was assumed to have "gone to Keptville."

L'ORIGNAL: A town cursed by a French copy editor. In 1802, Jean de Crayon-Bleu is said to have cackled, "This will drive those anglais editors at Canadian Press mad forever, by gar." Ever since then reporters and broadcasters have been referring to the town as "L'Original".

WELLAND: The famous trader Thorold Dunnville de Pelham earned the town this name. In dealing with American liquor importers across the

Niagara River, he countered every offer with, "Well, and what else?" He became known as "Welland de Pelham" and the nickname was applied to this trading post in the 1840s.

STITTSVILLE: 'Tis said that on the original stagecoach line from Carleton Place to Ottawa, inebriated drivers sometimes announced their stop at a tavern here as "'stitsville." Male passengers were delighted to spend some time at the bar with the entertaining tavern keeper, the well-endowed Jennifer Audrey Tooboobie.

STRATFORD: When early English explorers first reached Western Ontario, they encountered a strange rite practised by the Thespian tribe of Indians. This tribe had constructed a huge tent beside a slow meandering stream, and in the tent they conducted a weird nightly ritual. First, the whole village would re-enact the previous year's events. Then, the tribe would act out its wishes for the coming year. The English were so struck by the scene that they called the place Stratford, in honor of the tribal leader, Chief Shaking Spear. Out of respect for the Indians' talents, the Englishmen built a ticket booth. Eventually they fired all the Indians, imported English actors, and became rich.

LONDON: Named by a bunch of totally forgettable people who had absolutely no sense of imagination. Most of them became provincial politicians.

WATERLOO: When Napoleon passed through here, he was overcome by a strange sense of imminent disaster. "It might be the stench of frying German sausages, or it might be the proximity of English in London," he is reported to have said. "In any case, the place gives me the creeps." At the time of his visit the community was called Corsica Corners; after his defeat in Europe it was renamed Waterloo in jest.

KITCHENER: A mispelling of Berlin.

BERLIN: An archaic form of Kitchener

SWASTIKA: Swas-TEEK-a, not SWAS-tika. SWAS-tikas are symbols of Aryan pure idiocy. Swas-TEEK-as are symbols of Northern pure obstinacy.

Successful Military Campaigns of the War of 1812

Places in Ontario
Not Fit for a Queen

On her journeys through the strange and foreign land of Ontario, the Queen has toured a few wonderful points of interest. She has also toured a few ludicrous locations as well. Not only is there something mysterious about the choice of places she visits, there is something equally fascinating about the places she chooses not to see.

Now, for the first time, Ontario's coordinator of Queenly tours reveals why Her Maj refuses to be dragged to certain Ontario towns. Royal T. Charters provided this list on condition that his name not be used. So, when you discuss this list, don't use his name.

BATH: The Queen thinks she should not be seen in bath.

BALDERSON: The Queen never tours cheese factories. Constitutionally, she finds cheese tours binding.

CARLSBAD SPRINGS: The Queen never visits anything bad. If she wanted bad springs she'd 'av stayed in the royal bed.

CARP: The Queen may politely disagree, but she never carps. (Printer: beware of typo here).

CARRYING PLACE: The Queen gave up physical labor with the arrival of Edward.

DON MILLS: The Queen has trouble enough staying awake in Ottawa without trudging through Don Mills.

DRUMBO: The Queen has a phobia of flying elephants.

DRYDEN: The Queen has no interest in retired goaltenders.

EAR FALLS: The Queen is disgusted by the sound of one ear falling.

ECHO BAY: The Queen never talks to herself, although the Duke is interested in visiting here.

FROGMORE: The Queen saw quite enough in Quebec, thank you.

GRASSY NARROWS: The Queen fears the local mercury deposits will tarnish the royal jewels.

HOLLAND LANDING: The Queen believes in keeping The Netherlands up in the air on all matters.

HORNEPAYNE: The Queen already suffers from over-exposure to bagpipes.

IPPERWASH: The Queen always bathes her ippers in private (*see* Bath).

KILLALOE: The Queen is a patron of the British Save-a-loo Society.

KING CITY: The Queen refuses to go near this chauvinist community.

LEAMINGTON: The Queen grows her own tomatoes at home.

LITTLE BRITAIN: The Queen will not be insulted by a diminution of Great Britain.

MARATHON: The Queen does not indulge in long-distance running.

MOOSE FACTORY: The Queen does not care much for live moose, let alone seeing how they are made.

L'ORIGNAL: The Queen does not find French moose any improvement.

NEWBLISS: The Queen finds this proposition tempting but remembers that she is a married woman.

NEWCASTLE: The Queen can hardly afford the ones she already has.

OWEN SOUND: The Queen prefers not to inspect certain parts of the elephant of Ontario.

PORCUPINE: The Queen is sharply aware that procupines are death on Corgis.

PUCE: The Queen is never seen in puce.

SCOTLAND: The Queen comes to Canada to avoid Scotland.

SMITHS FALLS: The Queen fears a tour of the local chocolate factory. The Queen has not toured a chocolate factory since the mix-up at the Ex-lax plant in Brisbane.

TINCAP: The Queen feels that this is a slighting reference to her crown.

TUPPERVILLE: The Queen abhors Tupperville parties.

TWEED: The Queen prefers English tweed.

UNDERWOOD: The Queen cannot get keyed up about tours of typewriter factories.

WAWA: The Queen does not care for the goose.

Great Ontario Inventions

TOTEM POLES: Created by the Tote 'em Indian tribe of the Nipissing region. This tribe was named by early white explorers because they carved their famous ceremonial poles from Ontario white pine and toted 'em all the way to the West Coast by birch-bark freighter canoes. The vertical format of the totem figures represents man's eager attempts to catch the first rays of morning light as the sun rises above the ocean. The Tote 'ems had a wretched sense of direction and wound up on the wrong coast. When the Tote 'ems realized their mistake, they sold the remaining two untoted poles to the Royal Ontario Museum.

KAYAKS: These slender canoes were devised by early Torontonians for easier and safer transport down the Don River. The thin shape of the hull swiftly parted the rafts of sewage sludge floating on the river's surface. Eskimoes imported the kayak to the Arctic in the early 18th century.

OIL WELL: Canada's first gusher came in at Petrolia. Oil from this well was sold at cost to westward-bound pioneers, as Ontario's contribution towards the settlement of Saskatchewan and Alberta. The principle of sharing resources was maintained decades later, as Albertans returned the favor by selling Western oil at cost—the cost of Libyan oil.

BASKETBALL: Invented by James Naismith of Almonte. Naismith, an unemployed electrician, was experimenting with the old toss-the-cards-into-a-hat pastime. He used a marble and a galvanized three-foot-wide wash tub. He rarely missed. Television producers changed the game dramatically, demanding a ball big enough to be seen on the tiny screen and a basket without a clang.

RED RIVER CART: Designed and constructed at Kenora by Les Pionniers Frères for sale to Manitoba-bound settlers. These carts were infamous for their squealing axles. Historically-minded mechanics claim this was because the Pionniers brothers wrote their maintenance instructions in French. Nobody moving to Manitoba could read French manuals. The Pionniers doomed themselves to bankruptcy when they installed metric speedometers on the carts.

GREEN GABLES: Originally an ordinary two-room shack slapped together on a weekend near Bloomfield in Prince Edward County. Folklore gradually transferred it, adding gable after gable, to Prince Edward Island.

Psychologists say this represents a deep primeval urge of Central Canadians to return to the sea.

SEAL HUNT: At one time the biggest harvest in all of Ontario. Hundreds of thousands of seal pups were slaughtered in Georgian Bay in the late 1800s. An admirable body of angry European stage comedians, led by Brigitte de Poof-poof, denounced the slaughter in the theatre mags. A garden group from Collingwood, calling themselves Green Peas, attacked a sealing ship out of Midland with hoes and leaf rakes. The Government of Ontario banned the hunt in 1909, after conducting a poll which revealed that 50.0001 per cent of the population opposed sealing. Besides, the last seal had died in 1908.

PABLUM: Originally created at Toronto's Hospital for Sick Children as a nutritional breakfast for babies. In the early 1940s industrial espionage spies from the Ontario Progressive Conservative Party stole the recipe. Since the party's election to power in 1943, Pablum has been an essential ingredient of every speech made by an Ontario Premier. Medical researchers speculate there is a link between Pablum and Conservative longevity, not to mention long-windedness.

AUTOMOBILE: No car was ever invented in Ontario. What was invented in Ontario was stealing. The idea of the auto was stolen from inventors in other provinces. Ontario built auto factories and sold cars back to those provinces. Later Japan stole this idea. Ontario took out a patent on auto theft and tried to block Japanese imports.

TELEPHONE: Invented accidentally at Brantford as researchers looked for a use for a quarter. The first long-distance words were: "Hello? CRTC? Dr. Bell here. I want a rate increase."

STREETCAR: In 1883, a Toronto inventor installed electric lights inside horse-drawn carriages. He rigged up a system of overhead electric wires, and plugged in the cars. Unfortunately, all the horses were immediately electrocuted. Commuters were delayed for several hours until the TTC could find some electric motors that would fit the harnesses.

BICYCLE: The first bicycle was ridden in the sand dunes of Point Pelee by Orville Wrong, assisted by his brother Wilbur. The Wrongs, having failed to interest anyone in their airplane, put the world on two-wheelers.

AIRPLANE: Ontario builds airplanes to scare federal governments. The Avro Jetliner, the first commercial jet built in North America, was scrapped by a federal Liberal government. The Avro Arrow, a sleek and fast fighter aircraft, was shot down by a Conservative government. Ontario is currently working on a flying hot air and steam bicycle, in case the New Democrats ever come to power.

SUBMARINE BASE: In 1941, the federal government was looking for a safe and secure submarine haven, away from the German wolf packs off the east coast. Exercising its usual caution, it chose a small bay on Lake Couchiching, near Orillia. Half a dozen submarines were built on site, but the project was abandoned when the submarines rolled off the cable car at the Big Chute Marine Railway.

APPENDIX II

O'French's Terrific Trivia Quiz

O'French's Terrific
Trivia Quiz

1. A "granger" was (a) a green ranger, (b) a grass ranger, (c) a rangy ganger, (d) someone who felt at home on the grange, (e) an organization of range tenders.

Answer: (e). It was originally a secret farm organization, born in the United States, called the National Grange of Patrons of Husbandry. It eventually became a farmers cooperative and lobby group in Ontario.

2. In the first Ontario legislature, John Sandfield Macdonald was premier and Edward Blake was leader of the opposition. The two men had in common: (a) a cold, (b) a seat in the grange, (c) two elected seats, (d) a yacht at Ontario Place, (e) a summer cottage on Georgian Bay.

Answer: (c). Both were elected simultaneously to the House of Commons in Ottawa and to the Ontario Legislature.

3. In 1866, "City Arabs" in Toronto referred to (a) Lebanese restaurateurs, (b) homeless and unemployable young people, (c) real estate entrepreneurs, (d) visiting oil sheiks, (e) a Muslim church congregation on Bathurst Street.

Answer: (b).

4. At one time there were common schools and grammar schools. Grammar schools were: (a) correctional institutions for retraining wayward grandmothers, (b) special classes for students who couldn't spell grandma, (c) private schools for the wealthy, (d) correctional colleges for English teachers.

Answer: (c).

5. Oliver Mowat holds a record for: (a) writing the most books about whales, (b) building boats that wouldn't float, (c) living among wolves, (d) starring in a hit stage musical about himself, (e) running Ontario, (f) ruining Ontario.

Answer: (e). He was premier for 24 years, from 1872 to 1896.

6. During the 1890s, an English traveller described an Ontario city as "the prettiest, cleanest, healthiest and best conducted" he had visited

in North America. He was writing of (a) Hamilton, (b) Sudbury, (c) Windsor, (d) Toronto, (e) Cornwall.

Answer: (a). Maybe he was from Liverpool.

7. Model schools were: (a) paper schools stuffed with fireworks and burned on May 24, (b) correctional schools for errant models, (c) euphemisms for houses of ill repute, (d) crash courses in teacher training, (e) hobby clubs for tiny trains.

Answer: (d). Thirteen weeks of training told teachers all they needed to know to instruct the illiterate masses.

8. The Ross Bible was: (a) a set of daycare rules designed by George Ross, minister of education in 1883, (b) quotations from the scripture to be used in schools, (c) a wedge between Catholics and Protestants, (d) a list of plumbing regulations designed by Works Minister Ross (Leaky) Fawcett.

Answer: (b), which was unacceptable to everyone, causing (c). It was soon withdrawn.

9. The Protestant Protective Association was: (a) an insurance company insuring Anglican churches, (b) a supplier of jockstraps for church hockey leagues, (c) an anti-popery organization, (d) a false front for the IRA.

Answer: (c). Religious feelings ran high in the 1890s.

10. Orlando Q. Guffy was: (a) a songwriter, (b) an MPP, (c) a bartender at the Babes-in-Arms, (d) a writer, (e) premier of Ontario 1897–1899, (e) an airport in Florida.

Answer: (b) and (d), sort of. Orlando Q. Guffy was a fictional MPP whose column appeared in the satirical magazine *Grip*.

11. The Ontario version of the Women's Christian Temperance Union was born: (a) in a bar room, (b) in a brothel, (c) in Owen Sound, (d) in despair, (e) in Parry Sound, (f) in *Grip*.

Answer: (c), in 1874.

12. In the last century women were classed the same as imbeciles and insane people when: (a) riding trolleys, (b) drinking in bars, (c) using libraries, (d) voting, (e) debating with men.

Answer: (d). None of them were allowed to vote until 1917.

13. If you were to swim directly west from Niagara-on-the-Lake, you

would: (a) skin your knees on the Queen Elizabeth Way, (b) make like a migrating salmon over Niagara Falls, (c) risk a speeding ticket from the Buffalo police, (d) risk your life in Hamilton Bay, (e) bring greetings to the mayor of Oakville.

Answer: (d). You'd really have to like swimming a lot.

14. A British visitor said of an Ontario wonder, "It will always be what it is, only larger." He was talking of: (a) the government's deficit, (b) Niagara Falls, (c) Fenelon Falls, (d) Canada's Wonderland, (e) Toronto, (f) E.P. Taylor's bank account.

Answer: (e). A man of discerning taste, no doubt.

15. Stephen Leacock's fictional town of Mariposa was really: (a) a code word for marijuana, (b) derived from the Wild West town of Merry Posse, (c) an anagram of his lover's name, Prim Oasa, (d) discovered while he was in the shower using Mair Soap, (e) a slight mis-spelling of Orillia.

Answer: (e).

16. Blondin was: (a) the world's first hair dye, created in Dundas, (b) an 1890 proposal to extend Bloor Street to London, Ont., (c) the first man to arrive in Ontario on a rubber raft, (d) the first man to arrive in Ontario on a hang glider, (e) the first man to arrive in Ontario on a tight-rope, (f) the original name of the Blondie comic strip, conceived in Goderich.

Answer: (e). He was a French aerialist who tripped the light fantastic on a tight-rope strung across the Niagara Gorge.

17. Tiny, Tay, and Flos were: (a) early settlers of Simcoe County, (b) engineers who surveyed Simcoe County, (c) barmaids at the Waverley Hotel in the 1890s, (d) dogs, (e) win, place, and show entries in the 10th race at the 1900 Waverley Fall Fair.

Answer: (d). They were pet dogs of Lady Sarah Maitland, wife of Lieutenant-Governor Sir Peregrine Maitland, although locally believed to be the dogs of Lady Simcoe, who was no Lady but a mere Mrs. The village of Waverley is located on the corners of three townships named after those mutts (it's a three-dog town).

18. Lord Simcoe was: (a) the first governor of Upper Canada, (b) the first dog-catcher in Simcoe County, (c) the mayor of Simcoe, Ont., (d) a hotel in Toronto, (e) a character in Ontario mythology who helped Lady Simcoe train dogs.

Answer: (d), a fanciful commercial name which led to the establishment of (e).

19. The Laird of MacNab was: (a) a hotel in Scotland, (b) the last chieftain of the MacNabs, (c) a feudal lord of the Ottawa Valley, (d) a brand of scone, (e) a Scottish retreat in Glengarry County.

Answer: (b) and (c). Driven from Scotland in 1823, Archibald MacNab re-established his fiefdom in MacNab Township in Renfrew County.

20. Sir Harry Oakes, the Kirkland Lake mining magnate, painted the roof of his mansion green with: (a) punk hair dye, (b) nail polish, (c) urine, (d) vegetable dye, (e) pickle juice.

Answer: (c). He collected urine from his miners and used it to wash his new copper roof, hurrying the natural oxidation process to turn the roof green. Later Sir Harry died.

21. The victim in the last fatal duel in Ontario died from: (a) blinking in a staring match, (b) boredom in a Legislative speaking contest, (c) exhaustion in a paint-drying marathon, (d) a sharp paper dart in a Legislative committee, (e) a pistol ball.

Answer: (e), at Perth, in 1833.

22. One of the early critics of Ontario Hydro was: (a) Sir Sandford Fleming, (b) Sir Adam Beck, (c) Lady Simcoe, (d) Mitch Hepburn, (e) Darcy McKeough.

Answer: (d). He was accused of throwing an apple at the hat of (b), who founded Hydro, and left high school under the threat of electrocution. Later he became premier of Ontario and auctioned off cabinet limousines, but not Ontario Hydro.

23. At Jones Falls, John By the royal ditch-digger built something which was the biggest of its kind in North America at the time. This was: (a) a hole in the ground, (b) a lock, (c) a key, (d) a dam, (e) a lake, (f) a deficit, (g) a tavern.

Answer: (d), a stone horseshoe-shaped dam, built without mortar and twice as high as any dam on the continent at the time (1830).

24. The K and P was: (a) an early Ontario chain of supermarkets, (b) a short form for Kingston Penitentiary, (c) a short form for "kick and push", (d) a short-lived railway, (e) a pioneer sauce for steak and sausage.

Answer: (c) and (d). The Kingston and Pembroke Railway, known locally as the Kick and Push, ran from Kingston to Renfrew.

25. Nancy was (a) a bad, bad girl in Thorold, (b) a very good girl in Prescott, (c) a tigress, (d) a scorpion, (e) a warship, (f) a comic strip character sketched in Galt.

Answer: (e), a British warship sunk in the Nottawasaga River in the War of 1812. The Tigress and the Scorpion were American warships.

26. Sunshine, Egypt, Randwick, and Henfryn were: (a) partners in York's first law firm, (b) four forgettable premiers of Ontario, (c) clearings in the Queen's Bush, (d) Indian chiefs who sold Sudbury to the whites, (e) brands of illicit whiskey produced during prohibition.

Answer: (c). They are ghost towns in the Grey and Bruce counties, an area known at one time as the Queen's Bush.

27. The infamous Donnellys of Lucan were murdered en masse because: (a) they hadn't paid their hydro bill, (b) they were chain-smokers, (c) they talked loudly, (d) they were the wrong kind of Irish, (e) they were bad actors.

Answer: (e) on the stage of life, but there was a strong element of (d) in a religious feud transplanted from Ireland.

28. Catharine Parr Trail was: (a) the road to the St. Catharines Golf Course, (b) the author of *Roughing It In The Bush*, (c) a West Coast landscape painter, (d) the author of *The Female Emigrant's Guide*, (e) the first female news reader on CBC television.

Answer: (d), in 1854, to assist new arrivals in the wilds of Ontario. *Roughing It In The Bush* was written by her sister, Susanna Moodie.

29. Hariot Georgina Rowan Hamilton became: (a) the discoverer of Hamilton, (b) Lady Dufferin, (c) Mrs. Frederick Temple Blackwood, (d) goddess of the Hamilton Tiger-Cats, (e) a terrible bore.

Answer: (c) first, then (b) when Mr. Blackwood became Lord Dufferin and Governor-General of Canada, and later (e) in her writing style.

30. The first UFO in Ontario: (a) kidnapped the government, (b) seized control of Ontario earthlings, (c) didn't stick around on earth very long, (d) vanished into the night.

Answer: All of the above. UFO stood for the United Farmers of Ontario and was elected as a "farmers' government" in 1919. It didn't last long.

31. Whitby is the city of: (a) garlic, (b) onions, (c) rutabagas, (d)

marigolds, (e) petunias, (f) rhubarb.

Answer: (d), officially.

32. A man said, "I was sentenced to contend on the soil of America with democracy, and that if I did not overpower it, it would overpower me," He was: (a) Nikita Kruschev, (b) Ronald Reagen, (c) John Graves Simcoe, (d) Francis Bond Head, (e) Lord Durham, (f) Lee Harvey Oswald.

Answer: (d). He was governor of Upper Canada, 1836–38, when William Lyon Mackenzie and the lads were stirring up trouble about the Family Compact. Democracy overpowered Sir Francis.

33. In a strange alliance for a common cause, the Orange Lodge united with: (a) the IRA, (b) the Upper Canada Apple Pickers Union (UCAPU), (c) the Roman Catholics, (d) the Fenians, (e) the Purple Gang, (f) the Masons.

Answer: (c), in 1836, to defeat the reformers who were threatening to bring democracy to Upper Canada.

34. The trillium was adopted as Ontario's official flower under the administration of: (a) John Graves Simcoe, (b) Elizabeth Simcoe, (c) Oliver Mowat, (d) Mitch Hepburn, (e) William Davis.

Answer: (d), in 1937. Picking petals took Ontario's mind off the Depression.

35. The Oshawa strike was: (a) a screwball pitch invented by a sensational young pitcher, Tim Buck. (b) a pre-emptive sales strategy by General Motors to beat Ford in the fall, (c) a labor dispute displaying Premier Hepburn's true nature, (d) a patented method of assembling automobiles with hammer blows.

Answer: (c). He was prepared to break a strike at GM's Oshawa plant with policemen and hired mercenaries.

36. Tim Buck was: (a) a communist, (b) a flea in Hepburn's ear, (c) a burr under Hepburn's saddle, (d) a thorn in Hepburn's side, (e) a fly in Hepburn's ointment, (f) all of the above, and more.

Answer: (f). Tim Buck was head of the Communist party, which kept Mitch in stitches.

37. Mother Barnes was: (a) an owner of a winery, (b) a witch, (c) chairman of the Council on the Status of Women, (d) chairman of the Council on the Status of Witches, (e) chairman of the Council on the Status of Wineries.

Answer: (b), although not really. Mother Barnes was a woman with some clairvoyant powers who lived in Eastern Ontario in a village called Plum Hollow, and was known as The Witch of Plum Hollow.

38. Guelph is the: (a) Garden City, (b) Marigold City, (c) Queen City, (d) Royal City, (e) the Limestone City.

Answer: (d). (a) is St. Catharines, (b) is Whitby, (c) is Toronto, and (e) is Kingston.

39. Three types of professionals regularly graduate in one medium-sized Ontario city. They are: (a) doctors, (b) astronauts, (c) drivers, (d) soldiers, (e) dentists, (f) golfers, (g) criminals, (h) swimmers, (i) skiers.

Answer: (a), (d) and (g) from Kingston's Queen's University, Royal Military College, and various penal colonies. The institutions are color-coded.